## Praise for
## *The Good News About Marriage*

"In the thirty-two years I have been deeply immersed in the world of marriage ministry, I have been demoralized at times by the negative statistics quoted. And now I am ecstatic as I read the truth in this incredible book. Thank you, Shaunti, for doing the hard work necessary to expose the myths and lies and for finally revealing the facts about marriage. This book and the undeniable research in it is a game changer!"

> —JIMMY EVANS, founder and CEO of MarriageToday,
> senior pastor of Trinity Fellowship

"This is an important book. Shaunti and Tally do an impressive job of showing that there is room for different viewpoints on divorce statistics and room for optimism about marriage. I believe that people make higher-risk choices partly because they have lost hope in marriage, and this book presents a basis for real hope."

> —DR. SCOTT STANLEY, coauthor of *A Lasting Promise,*
> research professor at the University of Denver

"Lamenting the demise of the family has almost become a cottage industry. There's a lot of legitimate bad news out there, but Shaunti reminds readers that the situation might not be nearly as dire as we think—in fact, there are encouraging signs of hope. That's a welcome message!"

> —JIM DALY, president of Focus on the Family

"There are many bad stats out there about marriage, but Shaunti debunks those myths and provides clarity about marriage in general and how to strengthen your own marriage. *The Good News About Marriage* is well worth your time."

—ED STETZER, PhD, president of LifeWay Research

"Every Christian leader in America needs to read the groundbreaking, hope-filled research in this book. Then they need to recommend that everyone in their sphere of influence read it as well! This is one of the most important marriage books I've ever read, and it will change how all of us think and talk about marriage and divorce."

—LYSA TERKEURST, *New York Times* best-selling
author, president of Proverbs 31 Ministries

"This book is *great* news about marriage! Every pastor, coach, or counselor will find a new zeal for working with marriages after learning the truth about the state of marriage today. I cannot wait to have Shaunti share these truths with the Catalyst audience."

—TYLER REAGIN, executive director of Catalyst

"*The Good News About Marriage* offers an important word of encouragement to believers who wonder if faith makes a difference in modern married life. Believers who put their faith into practice— who worship together and pray together—are much more likely to enjoy stable and happy marriages. This is good news indeed."

—W. BRADFORD WILCOX, director of the National
Marriage Project, associate professor of sociology
at the University of Virginia

"Academically rigorous, honest, and refreshingly bold, this book will make you question what you've always heard about the bad news of marriage. A seminal work, this book could change the social narrative about marriage for generations. This is a must-read for academics, marriage educators, and couples alike."

—RON L. DEAL, director of FamilyLife Blended,
best-selling author of *The Smart Stepfamily*

"This groundbreaking research gives us a whole different framework to think about marriage, divorce, and relationships. This is fantastic material that provides powerful tools to help us improve our personal relationships and those in our communities."

—JUD WILHITE, author of *The God of Yes,* pastor
of Central Christian Church

"Shaunti's thoroughly researched book will inject life and hope, not only into our national consciousness about marriage, but also into every individual marriage in the country."

—DR. TIM CLINTON, president of American
Association of Christian Counselors, executive
director of Center for Counseling and Family
Studies at Liberty University

"Shaunti takes aim at marriage myths that have spread like cancer through our culture—myths that have become self-fulfilling prophecies. This book is packed with game-changing revelations! Bravo to Shaunti for her outstanding research."

—EMERSON EGGERICHS, best-selling author
of *Love and Respect*

"This is some of the most important information on marriage for this generation, and Shaunti brings practical inspiration on every page. This is the new go-to book for facts on marriages in America—and it's much better news than we often hear."

—DR. JIM BURNS, president of HomeWord, author
of *Creating an Intimate Marriage* and *Closer*

"You've read the bad news about marriage—the cohabiting couples, extramarital affairs, and soaring divorce rates. But this book shows there's a lot of good news about marriage today, and it's about time someone said so!"

—BOB LEPINE, co-host of *FamilyLife Today*

"It's impossible to overstate the importance of these findings. Our beliefs directly influence our actions, and our beliefs about marriage have been wrong. Shaunti and Tally provide genuine hope that is based on truth. This book changes everything."

—CHRISTOPHER MCCLUSKEY, best-selling author,
president of Professional Christian Coaching Institute

"Shaunti Feldhahn presents profound truth in the most relatable way. We have consistently used her books to help lay foundations for strong marriages in our church and to gain tremendous perspective about our own relationship. Now, in *The Good News About Marriage,* Shaunti gives us the gifts of a positive perspective and a practical strategy to make the most of our marriages."

—STEVEN AND HOLLY FURTICK, lead pastor of Elevation
Church, author of the *New York Times* bestseller *Greater*

# shaunti feldhahn
with tally whitehead

Foreword by Andy Stanley

# the
# good news
## about marriage

### Debunking Discouraging Myths
### About Marriage and Divorce

- the fallacy of the 50% divorce rate
- the surprising truth about divorce among churchgoers
- how most marriages are happier and healthier than we've been told

MULTNOMAH
BOOKS

The Good News About Marriage
Published by Multnomah Books
12265 Oracle Boulevard, Suite 200
Colorado Springs, Colorado 80921

Details in some anecdotes and stories have been changed to protect the identities of the persons involved.

Hardcover ISBN 978-1-60142-562-1
eBook ISBN 978-1-60142-563-8

Cover design by Kristopher K. Orr

Published in association with the literary agency of Calvin Edwards, 1220 Austin Glen Drive, Atlanta, Georgia 30338.

Published in the United States by WaterBrook Multnomah, an imprint of the Crown Publishing Group, a division of Random House LLC, New York, a Penguin Random House Company.

Multnomah and its mountain colophon are registered trademarks of Random House LLC.

Library of Congress Cataloging-in-Publication Data
Feldhahn, Shaunti Christine.
    The good news about marriage : debunking discouraging myths about marriage and divorce / Shaunti Feldhahn, with Tally Whitehead. — First Edition.
        pages cm
    Includes bibliographical references.
    ISBN 978-1-60142-562-1 — ISBN 978-1-60142-563-8 (electronic)  1. Marriage—Religious aspects—Christianity.  I. Title.
    B835.F45 2014
    261.8'3581—dc23

                                                            2013048609

Printed in the United States of America
2014—First Edition

10 9 8 7 6 5 4 3 2 1

Special Sales
Most WaterBrook Multnomah books are available at special quantity discounts when purchased in bulk by corporations, organizations, and special-interest groups. Custom imprinting or excerpting can also be done to fit special needs. For information, please e-mail SpecialMarkets@WaterBrookMultnomah.com or call 1-800-603-7051.

From Shaunti

*For Jeff:*
*The fact that I get to live with you over the*
*course of my lifetime is definitely the biggest*
*scam I've pulled off.*

• • •

From Tally

*For Eric:*
*You had me at hello.*

# Contents

# Foreword

When Shaunti first briefed me on what she was finding, I was staggered. As a pastor of a large church and someone who is passionate about strong marriages and families, I feel a responsibility to stay informed. Many of us do. And we think we are. We think our discouragement about the state of marriage in our culture is based on years of solid evidence.

If half of marriages today end in divorce, if most couples feel the fire go out after a few years, if the rate of divorce is the same in the church as it is out, then the institution of marriage is in trouble. We subconsciously revert to crisis mode. We talk widely about the need to work harder, to always be on the lookout for potential problems, to stick to our promises, and to endure hard marriages for the long haul—even when we want to quit.

And all those actions are important—*absolutely*. But when we act and speak in crisis mode, we become a small part of a very large problem: discouraging people about marriage instead of encouraging them.

In order for people to work harder, to want to prevent potential problems, and to stick to their promises, they need to believe they can make it. They need to believe they cannot just survive their marriages but they can enjoy them. They need to believe that their marriages can thrive.

And it turns out that hope is out there. We just didn't realize it. It turns out that we have been accepting the discouraging beliefs about the state of marriage without questioning. In these pages, Shaunti makes a good case that at least some of our conventional wisdom is based on false beliefs. She makes a good case that there are actually many good, solid, evidence-based reasons to be *encouraged* about the state of marriage and reasons to encourage others as well.

That being the case, we shouldn't talk about marriage and divorce as we have in the past. It is good news that there is good news out there! And I look forward to telling people that good news about marriage.

—Andy Stanley
Senior Pastor
North Point Ministries

# Surprising News About Marriage

## What Most People Don't Know...but Need To

I n 2006 I was writing one of my newspaper opinion columns and referencing the high prevalence of divorce. I wanted to correctly cite the most recent divorce rate but was confused by conflicting sources and articles. After trying to figure it out for two or three hours (a lifetime in the newspaper business), I tossed it to my then research assistant (now senior researcher) Tally Whitehead, so I could keep working on the column. But after several more hours, Tally came back even more perplexed than when we started.

*It can't be this difficult,* I thought. We quickly called a respected expert on marriage and divorce and asked, "What's the exact divorce rate?"

Her unexpected answer: "No one knows."

*Huh?* Before I could say anything, she continued, "And it depends on what you mean by the 'divorce rate.' There are many different types of divorce rates. There are also many different surveys, of different groups of people; there are different ways of tracking the rate of divorce today and projecting it in the future. They all say different things. There's no way to know one 'exact' rate."

"Well…" I tried to gather my flustered thoughts. "Just an estimate, then. Roughly what percentage of marriages will end in divorce? Like, what does the Census Bureau say?"

"The Census Bureau stopped projecting divorce rates in 1996. And even those projections were based on divorce increasing, and it's decreased instead. That won't help you."

"The divorce rate has decreased? Really? But it is still around 50 percent, right?" After all, I'd heard for years that half of all marriages end in divorce.

"Actually, the divorce rate has never hit 50 percent. It has never even gotten close. Again, it depends on what you mean by the divorce rate, but no matter what definition you use, we're significantly below 50 percent right now. It is maybe closer to 30 to 40 percent, but again, no one knows."

My first thought was *Nuts! I'm going to have to edit my column.*

My second thought was *But wait a minute. What? The divorce rate has never gotten close to 50 percent? Why haven't we heard this before? That's a really big deal!*

That was eight years ago. And only gradually over the next few years did I begin to realize what a big deal the truth actually was—not only about that, but about several other marriage and divorce myths. Myths that are very discouraging…and very common.

## Why It Matters That We Get to the Truth

As part of the relationship research that my husband, Jeff, and I have done over the past twelve years, we have interviewed and surveyed thousands of people about their innermost thoughts, needs, and fears. Early on, we began to get a clear window not only into their needs as men and women, which was what we were primarily trying to study, but also into how their relationships worked, what inspired and discouraged them, what they believed about marriage, parenting, the workplace, and culture.

Eventually it was clear that there was one common denominator among marriages that survived versus those that failed: hope. There were many different factors that led to either outcome, of course. But underneath it all was this bottom line: Did the couple have a sense of hope…or a sense of futility?

A couple could go through a terrible period, but if they felt certain they would make it, they usually did. Even if a couple lacked that certainty, the hope that things *could* get better was often enough to keep them going. With a feeling of *We can get through this,* they would do what was needed to right the ship, patch the holes, and keep sailing.

But if a couple instead thought *This is never going to get better* or *We're not going to make it,* they usually seemed to have a different outcome. A sneaking feeling of futility took over and with it a sense of inevitability. They assumed things would never change, even if they wanted them to. Instead of motivating the couple to fight harder for their marriage, their belief in approaching doom had the opposite effect. After all, if the ship is going to sink anyway, why bother working so hard to bail it out? Far better, they think, to work on escaping the wreck intact.

In other words, a couple's futile feeling *We aren't going to make it* ends up being one of the main reasons they don't make it.

> A couple's futile feeling that *We aren't going to make it* ends up being one of the main reasons they don't make it.

Those who work directly with troubled couples—counselors, therapists, clergy, and marriage mentors—told me they generally agree. If even one spouse has a sense of hope that things can change, or simply a vision to keep going no matter what, it is amazing how often that one-sided commitment keeps the marriage afloat long enough to get it sailing again. But it is tough to overcome both spouses having a sense of futility.

## The Big Cultural Problem

The problem is that we have a culture-wide sense of futility when it comes to marriage, a feeling that, as you will see in the following chapters, is based on conventional wisdom that simply isn't true!

I hear it everywhere. A sense of discouragement about marriage, and the evidence that seems to justify it, saturates our culture. The idea that half of all marriages end in divorce, for example, is accepted as fact.

For years, and with all good intentions, we have been thinking and talking about marriage as being in trouble. We comment on the "unhealthy" state of our unions and the "skyrocketing rate of divorce." I cannot count the number of times I myself have referenced the 50 percent divorce rate from the stage in my marriage conferences! Many books, TV shows, radio programs, speeches, and sermons also discuss just how often happiness fades in marriage. Married couples talk about beating the odds, while live-in couples ponder, *Why should we bother getting married?* And in the process we are absorbing a vastly inflated sense of futility. Because although there are indeed plenty of legitimate concerns about marriage, there are others—a lot of others!—that are closer to myth than reality.

I am guilty of spreading every one of those myths myself. But not anymore. After an eight-year investigative study, I now know that although there *are* plenty of challenges, most marriages are still far stronger, happier, and longer lasting than most of us realize. It is so important for us to get that truth out there because, as mentioned earlier, the belief otherwise can become a self-fulfilling prophecy.

Another consequence of our cultural discouragement is that many couples avoid marriage altogether for the same reason. I recently read an excerpt of a popular book, *This Is the Story of a Happy Marriage,* in which the author explained why she avoided marrying her boyfriend for eleven years: "By not marrying Karl, we could never get divorced. By not marrying him, he would never be lost to me."[1]

After years of interviews and surveys, I have heard this type of fatalistic reasoning more times than I can count, and it is undoubtedly one reason for some of the cultural concerns that *are* accurate and that worry those who care about marriage. For example, more people today *are* living together as their first step, instead of or before marrying.[2] More than four in ten children *are* being born to unmarried women.[3] And one reason for these trends is the sheer number of people who think getting married is futile.

Those who work directly with couples are just as concerned as the couples themselves. I know I sure used to be, as I would speak at a marriage conference, look out over the audience, and wonder how many of them would be divorced in a few years.

And in the church community where I often do those marriage conferences, I find that pastors, priests, and counselors are even more discouraged. They, after all, are often the ones most likely to be contacted when a marriage goes wrong. I can no longer count the number of pastors who have expressed, "It is so discouraging to marry a young couple and know that they have only a one in two chance of making it."

And it's not just in the Judeo-Christian world that clerics are troubled. After seeing in a church conference advertisement that I would be sharing my research about the small things that make a big difference in marriages, a local Muslim imam came for the day to take notes. Afterward, we spent some time talking, and he explained his concerns for those he ministers to:

> In my community, we have a lower divorce rate, I think. But that doesn't mean we have a better feeling about marriage. It doesn't mean we have figured out how to do marriage well. We have many couples from other countries; some are in arranged marriages. Traditionally, a couple gets married expecting to be together for life, whether or not they are happy. But now, here [in America], that isn't enough. Usually a family is here because they want the American pursuit of happiness. They see it on TV and they want that great life, that good marriage, but don't always know *how*. And they don't always have the structure around them to help—the grandparents or the friends. And when one person in our community gets divorced, they worry that they will be next. They need this encouragement that they can make it.

## Bad News Isn't Motivating

Thinking that there is so much turmoil in marriage, those who work with marriages—therapists, clergy, writers, or speakers like me—are caught between a rock and a hard place. We feel we have to get across just how seriously the couple has to take the situation and how hard they may have to work, but we know that doing so could potentially discourage the couple before they start.

One pastor told me, "I do premarital counseling and require a couple to have three sessions with me before they get married. When I begin premarital counseling, I start off with the fact of reality. 'Do you know how many people get divorced? It's about 50 percent. That's discouraging, but you need to face the facts that marriage is not easy. So you need to get this education.'"

But instead of seeing the couple being motivated to work hard, he sometimes sees a damaging fear set in instead. Here's how he put it: "The thought that the divorce rate is 50 percent can be very, very discouraging and frightening. Especially when someone actually starts struggling, they are so wrapped up in their emotional experience that they aren't thinking right then, and it's easy to just say, 'It's a slippery slope, so why fight it?'"

Essentially, the subconscious bad-news beliefs about marriage and divorce are like a slow-acting poison. It is not that a couple starts out halfway expecting to fail (although that might be the case for some). Most start out believing—truly believing—that they will beat the statistics. *We're going to be in the 50 percent that make it,* they think on their glorious wedding day. But the first time they have a major string of arguments, some start worrying. Somewhere down deep they start thinking that they might be in the wrong half, after all.

If things get worse and they don't know how to make it better, all they see is pain ahead. Eventually many believe they've passed the point of no return and will be one of the statistics, and they give up. They think, *Well, 50 percent of other marriages couldn't make it either.* And they don't realize that those particular statistics are erroneous and that there is no inexorable downward pull to the ending of a marriage, as if gravity were pulling water down a bathtub drain. They don't realize that most marriages *are* doing well and that it is very likely that theirs can survive this hard time and thrive again. All they can see is the pain.

Here's how one woman put it when she was sharing with me the situation surrounding her divorce four years before:

> It's a season of crisis when making the decision to split— you just want the pain to end. You will grasp at anything to justify it. It is only later that the consequences to you and your family—your kids—become clear.
>
> If I thought divorce was much more rare, especially in the church, I would have worked harder. I think the 50 percent statistic makes it easier to just give up and divorce. People like me view our divorce as a painful failure, but when supposedly 50 percent fail anyway… well…failing doesn't seem so bad because you have a lot of company.

Think how different it would be if a friend could honestly tell a struggling couple, "I know it is hard right now, but statistically you're going to be just fine." Or how different it would be if the struggling couple felt *This isn't the end of the world. We'll get through this because most couples do.* Or how different it would be if an unmarried couple who was unsure about the benefit of marriage knew that most marriages not only survive but thrive.

## The Good News

By the end of this book, I hope you'll agree that despite some real concerns, there is also a great deal more good news out there than many of us have believed before—and that knowing it changes everything. In the chapters that follow, I will confront five demoralizing myths about marriage and show you these five good-news truths instead:

1. The actual divorce rate has never been close to 50 percent.[4] It's significantly lower and has been declining over the last thirty years.

2. Most marriages aren't just so-so. The vast majority are happy.

3. The rate of divorce in the church is not the same as among the non-churchgoing population. It too is significantly lower.

4. Remarriages aren't doomed. A significant majority survive and thrive.

5. Most marriage problems aren't caused by big-ticket issues, so being in a marriage, or fixing a troubled one, doesn't have to be as complicated as people think. Little things can often make a big difference.

Will there be exceptions to the truths above? Yes, sadly, millions of them. And among the roughly sixty million marriages that currently exist in our country,[5] there are still too many that struggle. Some of the big-picture troubling issues surrounding the state of marriage are very real.

But we have spent years hearing about all the bad news. Everyone is all too aware that those problems are out there. What we often don't know is the very real good news or that some of the bad news isn't accurate. So that is what we will be focusing on in this book. This is not a measured, equal treatment of both sides. This is a rigorous, fair, and accurate attempt to reclaim a whole other side of the truth about marriage!

> This is a rigorous, fair, and accurate attempt to reclaim a whole other side of the truth about marriage!

## Important Points to Keep in Mind

Before we dive into what we found, let me emphasize a few key goals and caveats.

First, Tally and I are analysts, not statistical demographers. But we have made a good-faith effort in eight years and thousands of hours of research to investigate, understand, and bring to you what we view as the most representative, most important information in each of the five areas mentioned above. We also try to give you a quick primer for evaluating this type of data yourself as you go forward. But it is imperative to emphasize that this was an extremely complicated area of study, an inexact science, and a moving target.

Second, our ultimate goal wasn't just to uncover the precisely correct answer within a bunch of complex data (although we certainly tried to do so), but to reclaim one whole side of the story and, as a result, start a much bigger-picture conversation: Should we change how we think and talk about marriage and divorce? If people are discouraged by the mythical bad news, should we vocally celebrate the very real good news? But if we do so, what amount of sober realism is needed for people to take marriage seriously? And so on. Although Tally and I will inevitably hear from those who might disagree with this number or that percentage calculation, the reality is that *many* of the numbers in the pages ahead could be adjusted without changing the ultimate conclusion that there is a great deal of unrecognized good news about marriage out there, and we need a paradigm shift in how we focus on it.

Third, despite the challenges posed by the complexity of the research, we were extremely rigorous about the process. Because this book needed to counter the pull of contemporary myths, we went straight to the data, studies, and, wherever possible, to the researchers themselves and tried to stay clear of articles, reports, or comments drawn from the studies. This approach was necessary because we found that when we tried to track secondary articles or news stories back to the actual data source, there were dozens of cases where a well-intentioned journalist, analyst, or even marriage expert quoted key information incorrectly or even quoted studies that, it turned out, didn't exist. (I chuckled when one marriage leader said, "You're like Snopes for marriage!") We also found countless cases where a news story emphasized the small negative details and ignored the large positive ones. So we have made it our goal to always eyeball the actual research and examine the raw data in hundreds of studies. We have also had dozens of interviews, phone calls, and e-mail exchanges with the researchers behind many of these studies, the preeminent researchers in the area of marriage and divorce. I have personally met with the authors of several key studies you'll read about in these pages.

Yet, fourth, despite our best efforts, I am quite sure there will be legitimate questions about certain facts, our reasoning, or conflicting statistics that Tally and I might have missed. Again, we are making our best judgment, and even the experts who have been studying this for decades do not always agree with one another. And frankly, as that first expert told me in 2006, we have seen for ourselves that this is indeed an arena in which there often isn't one right answer. There can even be many different ways of looking at things within the same data set. New information will also inevitably arise after this book goes to print; in fact we actively hope it does, as researchers start investigating the positive data sets and not just the negative ones!

Ultimately, we simply think it is important for you to hear the truth we found in the numbers and see the very real, overwhelming evidence for some heartening conclusions about marriage, not just the discouraging ones you have heard up until now.

Yes, some very real bad news is out there. But the good news is out there too. And it can give some much-needed encouragement to marriages today. Remember the pastor quoted earlier, who was talking about the scariness of the current notions about a 50 percent divorce rate? After I shared with him the truths I was learning, here is what he concluded:

> This good news about marriage being stronger than we think—especially in the church—will be so helpful. It will be helpful for me as I work with couples who are thinking of getting married. It will be helpful for my counselors who work with couples in trouble. And it will be helpful also for the public. It will be such an encouraging thing to know that, despite everything we hear, we still can believe in marriage today.

*We still can believe in marriage today.* Yes we can. Get ready to dig in.

## Summary

- Much of the key divorce information in news articles and other common references is inaccurate or interpreted incorrectly, downplays the positive findings, or, in some cases, quotes studies that don't exist.
- People believe a lot of bad news about marriage— much of which isn't true—and there is a need for a paradigm shift, to reclaim the very real good news as well.

- Because there really is good, encouraging news, we need to seriously consider changing how we think and talk about marriage and divorce—not just discussing problems, but emphasizing the very real hope.
- The sense that *We probably won't make it* is itself one reason why some marriages *don't* make it. The couple thinks, *Well, at least we have a lot of company* instead of *Most marriages make it and we can too.* But if even one spouse believes there is hope, the marriage has a much better chance of surviving.
- Many people also avoid marriage altogether, thinking, *Why bother?*
- Although we know there is much more good news about marriage and divorce than we realized, getting to the truth is inexact and extremely complicated.

# 2

# Till Death Do Us Part

### How Most Marriages Actually Do Last a Lifetime

Let me introduce you to a young couple I met at a marriage conference a few years back. I will call them Joe and Jana, but they are like hundreds of other couples I've met—and perhaps you have too.

Married eighteen months and with no kids yet, Joe and Jana are still in the newlywed phase. They enjoy living in a little apartment in the city, working full time, and going out to eat or to the movies. As they spoke to me, they were still clearly in the first blush of new love: holding hands and leaning into each other.

A few minutes into our conversation, Jana said, "Being married has been so wonderful. I'm glad we did it. And I think we'll probably make it."

Her husband was nodding happily, but I was jarred.

"*Probably* make it?" I asked, casually. "Why just 'probably'?"

"Well, there's no guarantee, you know." Her sober words were a surreal counterpoint to her sweet smile and the tender way she held her husband's hand. "Not when half of all marriages *don't* make it. But we're the type to work hard, so I think we'll beat the odds."

"*There's no guarantee.*" "*Half of all marriages* don't *make it.*" "*I think we'll beat the odds.*" Most couples don't verbalize these impressions about marriage so forthrightly, but I've found that they are there underneath. And all too often they lead to the dangerous (usually subconscious) feeling of *probably.* Not *We'll be together for life and make it work, no matter what,* but...*probably.*

So ask yourself: What happens when Joe and Jana encounter some inevitable difficulties, pain, and heartache? Is their "probably" mind-set going to help or hurt their chances of staying together? Will thinking *Half of all other marriages don't survive either* make a breakup less likely? Or more? The answer is obvious. For too many couples, believing that half of all marriages end in divorce is a reason why some marriages end in divorce. Or even if a couple stays together, the subconscious worry about not beating the odds can still be damaging. One or both partners might hold back. Maybe they're on guard. Perhaps they keep separate bank accounts, just in case.

But the marriage union is designed to be all in, where a couple can be vulnerable, transparent, and forgiving—not on guard. The actions that come from being on guard create distrust, build walls, and sabotage marriages. They set in motion the very outcome the couple didn't want—an outcome that too often comes *because* it feels inevitable—because couples have a sense of futility when they most need hope instead.

There's a passage in the Bible that says that without a vision, people perish. And the irony is that the hope people need—the good-news truth that will give them strength to reclaim their marriage—is actually there. They just don't know it yet!

## The Hope-Worthy Truth About the Divorce Rate

In the pages ahead, we'll be bringing you good-news truths about the divorce rate that you need to know. By necessity, we will be simplifying an *extremely* complex field of study; it took us years to understand just this one topic enough to investigate and analyze it to any helpful degree.[6] And that is why we think it is important to give you not just our conclusions but some highlights of how we arrived at those conclusions. Both in these pages and in the FAQ section at the back of the book, we will provide a tutorial to help you cut through the confusion and evaluate any reports you may see in the future.

So to start, here are the four big-picture, good-news truths we think are most important (and which are, with a few exceptions, undisputed among most experts):

- Half of all marriages today are *not* ending in divorce; the overall prevalence of divorce is nowhere close to 50 percent and never has been.
- The divorce rate has been declining overall for years; it has declined substantially since its peak around 1980.

- Even the good-news averages don't tell the whole positive story. Several actions and patterns dramatically lower couples' chances of divorce even more.
- From the 1970s right up to today, many respected researchers continue to believe in and refer to a 40 to 50 percent divorce rate, but these are always *projections* based on assumptions about what will happen in the future, and although some higher-risk groups have certainly hit that projected divorce rate, the average has never come close.

So let's take a closer look at these four vital facts that can encourage many people.

### Fact 1: The Prevalence of Divorce Has Never Been 50 Percent

Although experts mean many different things by "the divorce rate," the most familiar and simple way of discussing it is to determine what percentage of marriages have ended in divorce. Put another way, of those today who have ever been married, what percent have been divorced? We can call this the "prevalence" of divorce or the "current" divorce rate (and although we'll share other ways of looking at divorce, this will be the main way we refer to divorce in this book). Although this rate is popularly believed to be 50 percent, it has never been close.

Let's take a quick look at the encouraging truth about first marriages and then look at what we know about the broader picture of *all* marriages in our culture.

### *Seventy-Two Percent of Those Who Have Ever Been Married Are Still Married to Their First Spouse!*

Right now, according to one of the most recent Census Bureau surveys, 72 percent of people who have ever been married are still married to their first spouse.[7] In other words, *more than seven out of ten people are still married to their first spouse.*

Can we conclude the remaining 28 percent are divorced? Nope! They could be either divorced *or widowed,* since that percentage includes everyone who was married until a spouse died! Although there is no way to break out just divorce versus widowhood from this data, we can make a back-of-the-envelope estimate. Since the same data shows that around 10 percent of women have ever been widowed, we can make an educated guess that around 25 percent of first marriages may have ended because of divorce rather than widowhood.

Importantly, that percentage has been stable for years. (See graph, next page.) The "still married to first spouse" number was slightly over 70 percent in 1996,[8] and we can infer a similar number from another type of census survey even back in 1985, which was close to the years of the highest divorce rates of 1980.[9] (Before the 1970s spike in divorce, at any one time about 85 percent of first marriages were still intact. Since then, the number has been about 70 to 72 percent.)

It is imperative to note that the actual rate of divorce (rather than widowhood) for first marriages could be even lower than our estimate of 25 percent. According to the most recent Family Needs Survey of 6,171 people conducted by the large family

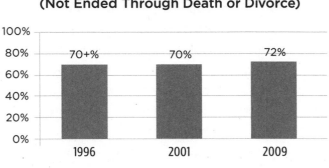

**Percent of First Marriages Still Intact (Not Ended Through Death or Divorce)**

Source: Census Bureau, 1996, 2001, 2009[10]

organization FamilyLife, of the marriages that were no longer intact, eight percentage points of that number were due to death rather than divorce![11] So theoretically, starting from our 28 percent of non-intact marriages, the average first-marriage divorce rate could be closer to 20 percent.[12]

Now, estimating that somewhere around 20 to 25 percent of first marriages end in divorce is still nothing to do handsprings about, but it is a whole lot better than the popular notion that the rate is double that!

### *Looking at Everyone (Including Those Married Multiple Times), Only Around Three in Ten Have Experienced Divorce*

Of course, discussing just first marriages doesn't give a full snapshot of society. Although you'll see in a later chapter that most remarriages last a lifetime as well, let's look at the current divorce rate for *all* marriages and, thus, society as a whole.

The broadest way to get a handle on this is to look at the many surveys that ask those who have ever been married a question like "Are you now or have you ever been divorced?"

At first glance, you might think this "ever divorced" number would be a simple, uniform assessment of the actual divorce rate. However, we found that this number swings widely depending on how the study is conducted and reported, which is one main reason for today's overall confusion and misunderstanding about the divorce rate. For example, a survey of divorce rates among women between the ages of eighteen and sixty will return a radically higher number than a very similar-looking survey of divorce rates among men between the ages of twenty-one and eighty. Nothing is simple in divorce land.

Furthermore, several highly publicized studies seem, on the surface, to suggest that nearly half of all subjects have ever been divorced. But when we looked at their methodology, none were a good reference for a national average.

For example, in the FAQ section in the back of the book, we discuss the Centers for Disease Control's data on marriage, from the National Survey of Family Growth, 2006–2010, which is regarded as a go-to report on divorce and very widely quoted. But it was primarily a study of fertility and heavily surveyed those who married very young. As you will see shortly, those couples typically have a much higher divorce rate, and because they are a very small portion of the married population, this study should *never* be used for the purpose of generalizing divorce rates. I am actually a bit stunned to see how many researchers have used those numbers wholesale to draw national conclusions!

Among the studies that are more representative for age at marriage, the "ever divorced" number for all marriages (not just first-time marriages) ranges from 23 percent to 37 percent, with a median around 32 percent.[13] In our judgment, the most authoritative of these studies is the Census Bureau 2009 Survey of Income and Program Participation (SIPP), which reveals a rate of 30.8 percent.[14] In other words, for society as a whole, among those who have been married, about three out of every ten have experienced divorce. Here is a quick list of several studies (some of which will be referenced again in later chapters).

## Survey Results: What Percent of Marriages Have Ended in Divorce?

| Study | Percent "Ever Divorced"* |
|---|---|
| US Census Bureau, 2009 SIPP (men and women; first marriage only) | <28% (probably less than 25%) |
| US Census Bureau, 2009 SIPP (women only; first or subsequent marriage)[15] | 30.8% |
| University of Chicago, General Social Survey, 2012[16] | 35.5% |
| University of Texas–Austin, National Fatherhood Initiative Marriage Survey, 2005[17] | 23.4% |
| Barna Group, 2008[18] | 33% |
| Marist Poll for the Knights of Columbus, 2010 (divorced or annulled)[19] | 37% |

*of those ever married

As we'll discuss in more detail in the FAQ section, the 30.8 percent "ever divorced" number (and others) is only a snapshot in time and is for society as a whole, not for individuals. Obviously if a survey taker were to survey a group of five thousand people one year and find that 30.8 percent were divorced, and then go back to that same group a few years later, more of that group would probably be divorced. Although an individual person's chance of getting divorced can only increase, not decrease, the bottom-line truth is still that the vast majority of people will not end up divorced.

For example, the same 2009 census study that found the 30.8 percent number also shows that even among one of the highest-risk age groups of baby boomers—women who were then between the ages of sixty and sixty-nine—only 37 percent had ever been divorced. Even better, nearly seven in ten of their *first* marriages were still intact![20] In other words, even among these high-risk age groups, most marriages *do* last a lifetime![21]

> Imagine the difference to our collective consciousness if we say "Most marriages last a lifetime" rather than "Half of marriages end in divorce."

Looking at how vastly different this truth is from what society believes, imagine the difference to our collective consciousness about marriage and divorce if we began to say "Most marriages last a lifetime" rather than "Half of marriages end in divorce."

And how encouraging it would be for people to know that, even better, the picture is only improving. Let's look at that next.

## Fact 2: The Divorce Rate Has Been Declining for Years

Most people have no idea that not only is the divorce rate not as bad as believed, but it has been declining for years.[22] One of the best ways to see this truth is to look at what is called the "crude divorce rate," which is the number of divorces per one thousand people. Because this number is based on municipalities' reporting of actual divorces, not projections or surveys, it is the best option we currently have for trying to understand an actual *trend* over time.[23]

After the introduction of no-fault divorce in the 1970s, there was a divorce boom as people rushed to take advantage of the fact that they could now get divorced just because they wanted to, without having to convince a judge there was a reason to grant it. But very quickly, people began to see the havoc this trend wrought, and the rush toward divorce cooled, hitting a peak around 1980 and then decreasing. In 1981, as you can see in the graph below, about 5.3 people out of every 1,000 got divorced, and that number has been falling overall since then, declining to 3.6 in 2011 (a drop of more than 32 percent overall).

There are additional key demographic reasons why divorce has continued to decline, and one of them is of particular concern for sociologists and society watchers. Today, more people are choosing to live together, either before they marry or instead of

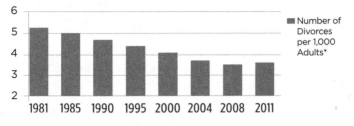

## The Declining Rate of Divorce Since the Peak Year

*Note: This "crude divorce rate" is the only one for which we have a complete apples-to-apples comparison over this length of time.[24]

Source: Census Bureau, Statistical Abstract 2012 (table 78) and CDC/NCHS National Marriage and Divorce Rate Trends (2011).[25]

tying the knot. As a recent study by Wendy Manning, Susan Brown, and Krista Payne at Bowling Green State University summarized, "Among women about three-quarters (74%) of first unions formed in the late 2000s were cohabiting in contrast to just over half (58%) 20 years earlier. The greatest increases in cohabitation as a first union appeared among working class women and men (high school graduates)."[26] The study also points out that overall, 60 percent of women had cohabited at some point between the ages of nineteen and forty-four.[27]

Since sociologists have found that cohabiting before marriage increases the risk of divorce later,[28] they speculate that those who cohabit would be the type to break up more easily if they *had* gotten married. Thus, one likely reason divorce is declining is simply that those folks are not getting married to begin with.

But another, and more positive, demographic reason for the

decline in divorce is that people are getting married later than they used to, and those marriages are simply more likely to last for a lifetime. (See discussion of the Dana Rotz study near the end of the chapter.)

### Fact 3: Certain Patterns and Actions Can Dramatically Change the Chance of Staying Married

There are a number of demographic factors and lifestyle choices that, statistically, quite dramatically reduce or increase a couple's chance of getting divorced. First, the demographic factors:

- *How old are the individuals when they get married?* Couples who marry in their midtwenties or later have a much greater chance of making it to their twentieth anniversary.
- *Do the individuals have a college education?* Statistically, college-educated people are far more likely to get married later and stick with their marriages.
- *Is it a first marriage?* First marriages appear to have a greater chance of success than subsequent marriages.
- *How long has the couple been married?* By and large, the greatest spike in divorces occurs not with the infamous "seven-year itch" but with those who never make it to their fifth anniversary.[29]

Now, that said, even those who are newlyweds, who get married young, who are on a second marriage, or who aren't college educated still have a great chance of having their marriage last a lifetime. But those who marry in their midtwenties or later, are college educated, and/or have already made it to the fifth anniversary of their first marriage find their chances of divorce dropping dramatically.

The highly respected researcher Andrew Cherlin has, for example, found that a college education alone drops the divorce rate to around one in six marriages (about 17 percent) for the first decade after the wedding.[30] And several other noted marriage researchers have informally told me that although the existing studies don't break it down this way, the divorce rate of people in those lower-risk categories could easily be as low as 5 to 10 percent.

> Although existing studies don't break it down this way, the divorce rate of people in lower-risk categories could easily be 5 to 10 percent.

One great example of this can be seen in a longitudinal study of residents of Framingham, Massachusetts, a small community where people tend to marry later and are more likely to have some college education. As a second wave to an earlier study, in 1971 researchers began tracking 5,124 adults and their marriages. Thirty years later, despite living through the divorce boom of the 1970s, only 9 percent of that group were divorced.[31] For many people reading this, that 9 percent divorce rate will look a lot like other communities around them where people don't tend to marry very young and where getting a college degree is a bit more common.

In some cases, in fact, depending on a few factors such as the longevity of the marriage, the divorce rate drops to almost zero. Although there has been much press about older couples divorcing, especially among the baby boomers who have significantly higher divorce rates, couples who have been married several decades have a minuscule chance of divorce. Well-known sociologist Scott Stanley, the author of *A Lasting Promise,* recently put it this way: "If two people have been married to each other for many years (let's say forty years or more) and it is the first marriage for both, the likelihood of their marriage ending in divorce is nil. Divorce is increasing rapidly among those older than fifty, but the great increase is among those who are remarried and/or in shorter duration marriages."[32]

Beyond the big-picture patterns mentioned above, various lifestyle choices, such as church attendance (see chapter 4), the decision to not live together before marriage, and/or being in community with supportive friends and mentors, drop the chances of divorce significantly as well.

For example, Dr. Stanley and his colleagues Howard Markman and Galena Rhoades at the University of Denver have spent years studying the implications of cohabitation. Stanley even pens a blog about the subject, aptly named *Sliding vs. Deciding,* reflecting the fact that couples who cohabit tend to slide into a long-term relationship and even marriage without making a decision of commitment prior to living together, which, as noted earlier, then increases the risk of divorce. This doesn't mean that couples who choose to cohabit are doomed, but it does mean that waiting until marriage to live together makes the marriage more likely to last a lifetime.

One case study of 143 couples fascinated me, because in many ways it covered several of these lifestyle factors that make a difference. Dan Chun, a senior pastor in Honolulu and the head of Hawaiian Islands Ministries, shared some important data arising out of his time as the singles pastor at a large California church. Plenty of the singles Dan worked with were in higher-risk groups, but he purposefully encouraged them to regularly attend church, meet each other in a healthy environment, be equipped with good teaching, avoid risky decisions like living together before marriage, and stay in a supportive community.[33] Of the many hundreds of singles he worked with between 1986 and 1992, there were 143 marriages. And as of the end of 2013, twenty-one to twenty-seven years later, only fourteen of those couples have divorced, less than 10 percent. Since all these marriages are well past the primary risk years, it is very possible that the rest of those marriages will stay intact for a lifetime.

In other words, instead of a 30.8 percent rate of divorce (as seen in the census numbers earlier), the divorce rate of those who stayed in a supportive community and so on was one-third of that! What Dan Chun did as a pastor, and what those couples did differently, is captured in his book *How to Pick a Spouse*.

As one noted researcher privately told me, "The magnitude of the shift in divorce is huge if you take a lower-risk path. That is just not in dispute."

## Fact 4: Experts Continue to Project a 40 to 50 Percent Divorce Rate—Which We've Never Hit

So, now, let's conclude this chapter by looking at one of the other main reasons why the notion of a 50 percent divorce rate has become so embedded in our culture: because we continue to see articles, studies, and sophisticated analyses by great researchers that seem to measure it that way.

Paul Amato at Pennsylvania State University, Scott Stanley at the University of Denver, Andrew Cherlin at Johns Hopkins University, and Kelly Raley at the University of Texas–Austin have all consistently said that the chance that a new marriage will end is between 40 and 50 percent.[34] The key word there is *will*. These are *projections,* not measurements. If a starry-eyed couple gets married today, what are their chances of getting divorced before they die? Or for people born in such and such a year, what are their chances of making it to their thirtieth anniversary, based on various demographic trends? Or what percentage of people in this ethnic group or that geographic region are likely to stay together for a lifetime?

This is where we get into complex projections far into the future, based on various assumptions. Although I am not an expert like these researchers, it looks like these assumptions may not have accounted enough for the positive trends we've seen. Ever since the divorce boom of the 1970s, several generations of researchers have predicted that the prevalence of divorce would be 50 percent or higher by now.[35] And yet divorce rates have been dropping instead, which is why we've never come close to the projected overall "ever divorced" rates we "should" have by now. The reality has always been more positive than what it was projected to be.

Now, certainly, there are some higher-risk groups that have hit a 50 percent divorce rate. But the *overall* projections don't seem to sufficiently take into account the fact that the crude divorce rate has dropped a lot since hitting a high in the 1979 to 1981 period. If projections had followed anywhere close to the same trend as the actual prevalence of divorce over the years, demographers would now be predicting something closer to a 33 percent divorce rate for a newly married couple.[36]

Again, that is a very simplified view, and demographers and social scientists have for years been running sophisticated analyses on complex life tables and data sets. In the end they may absolutely prove correct in their projections that an average of 40 to 50 percent of all new marriages will fail. But since we've never come close to hitting that...and divorce has steadily declined... I'm skeptical.

I'm also grateful that some of the experts themselves have been very open with us about this being an inexact science. During our research, Tally and I had an eye-opening conference call with Dr. Paul Amato, long considered one of the main authorities in this incredibly complex world of divorce demographics. In fact, several other researchers and experts I had interviewed had said things like "Well, I could see the projected divorce rate being 40 percent or lower, but Paul's number is 45 percent. And if Paul says that's what it is, that is good enough for me."

Yet Dr. Amato was forthcoming about the fact that *his* basis for saying 45 percent was a highly sophisticated analysis done by a now-retired Penn State professor named Robert Schoen, an analysis, it turns out, that wasn't just of divorce. Dr. Amato explained that Schoen's analysis was the best he'd seen (Tally and I had admired Schoen's work as well), but it was now dated (last data from 2000). Also, it wasn't projecting divorce for *new first* marriages but rather for *all* marriages, including the second and third marriages that have a somewhat higher rate of divorce. Even more important, and similar to the census data, Schoen's study also did not have a way of compensating for mortality; he could only analyze marriages ending, without knowing whether a marriage had ended because a couple divorced or one partner died. As Dr. Amato told us,

> So [today] we don't really know exactly what the projected rate is for first marriages. It's going to be lower than a 45 percent divorce rate. How much lower is not clear. It might be 40 percent. It could maybe be 35 percent; I don't know. So, if people are thinking the first time they marry, *I've got a fifty-fifty chance of staying married for the rest of my life,* that's too pessimistic.[37]

We agree with Dr. Amato and think that the projected rate of divorce for new first-time marriages is much more likely to be lower than current projections, especially if divorce rates continue to decline—which, a recent study says, is likely to be the case.

Dana Rotz, now a researcher with Mathematica Policy Research, undertook a massive project to examine the role of age in marriage and divorce while finishing her PhD at Harvard.[38] In e-mail correspondence with us, she explained that divorce rates are dropping so much that she projects that "compared to marriages beginning in 1979 or 1980 (perhaps the 'worst' years to marry in terms of the probability of divorce), marriages that began in 2008 will dissolve 40 percent less often."[39] She attributes 60 percent of that enormous drop directly to the fact that people are waiting longer to get married. And since there is little indication that most couples will suddenly begin marrying at the young ages that they did in our grandparents' era, divorce rates are likely to continue to decline.

## Phantom Myths, Real Hope

Regardless of what the real divorce rate is, the bottom line that nearly all researchers agree on is that the truth is not as bad as most people believe—and that the belief in the bad news is itself creating problems that didn't need to happen.

Dr. Stanley, one of the foremost researchers in this field (and who, like others, projects a 40 to 50 percent divorce rate), put it this way:

> I tell people that, yes, marriage is risky, and I believe
> this is accurate. Even if the divorce rate is less than the
> projections of 40 to 50 percent, it is still the most risky

thing that the greatest percentage of people will ever do. But people need to hear that non-marriage is even riskier. Living life in serial relationships, maybe having children outside marriage, will be harder.

Some people have identified marriage as the problem, and because they have this fear about marriage, they do things that *increase* their risks. Cohabitation is an example. They sample too much, trying to find the "right" partner. It's like a giant game of musical chairs. Marriage is seen as having all the costs, and cohabiting is seen as having no costs. Well you know what? It has a *lot* of costs.

For example, if you live together before you get engaged and married, it makes it more likely you'll get divorced. That's a big cost. It is a dumb thing to do, statistically. But people believe that they can improve their odds if they live together first. So some of the myths today about the risks of marriage lead to the very behaviors that decrease the odds of a marriage succeeding.

We do need to give people hope about marriage. The sense that they can do things to give them a future. The sense that they're going to make it. Marriage is an investment, and you want to know it has a future to invest in it.[40]

While I may take issue with various projections, the conclusion is universal: there is a great need for hope. Realizing the truth that divorce is *not* inevitable, that true hope is there, and that their marriages will probably last a lifetime gives struggling couples a vision for the future. Look at this comment from one woman who went through fire in her marriage and came out the other side:

> I have heard so many people over the years saying that the divorce rate in America is 50 percent. It's debilitating, and it turns out it's not even true. You can't listen to that. Instead, you need to assume your marriage *will* last.
>
> One of the thoughts that helped me to make it through my first pregnancy, fighting the fear of the coming pain that everyone tells you is the *worst pain ever,* was the thought that *Millions and millions of women over the centuries have successfully given birth, so I can do this too!*
>
> It is the same principle in considering making one's marriage last—*If so many others have succeeded, I'll keep trying and I will probably also succeed!*

What a difference it makes to reveal the assumptions of inevitability and futility for the lies they are, and know the good-news truth instead!

## Summary

- The current divorce rate is nowhere near 50 percent and has never been close to the 50 percent mark. Instead, the vast majority of marriages last a lifetime.

- According to the most recent authoritative data (2009 Census Bureau), 72 percent of people are still married to their first spouse. And of those who aren't, many were married for years until a spouse died. Based on various factors, we can estimate that perhaps 20 to 25 percent of first marriages have ended in divorce.
- Looking at all marriages (including second and third marriages) among women, just 30.8 percent have ended in divorce (2009 Census Bureau).
- The divorce rate has been declining, dropping 32 percent since its peak. According to other census data, the number of divorces per one thousand adults (the crude divorce rate) peaked in 1981 at 5.3 and has fallen to 3.6 as of 2011.
- Many factors dramatically affect the chances of divorce. Those who marry young (teens and young twenties), who don't go to college, who live together before marriage, and/or who do not attend religious services together have a higher risk of divorce. Those who get married in their midtwenties or later, go to college, don't cohabit first, and/or worship together could realistically have a 5 to 10 percent divorce rate.
- Top experts continue to project divorce rates of 40 to 50 percent, but these are future projections based on various assumptions, and we've never come close to that high of an overall divorce rate.

## Good News #1

The vast majority of marriages last a lifetime; the current divorce rate has never been close to 50 percent—it is closer to 20 to 25 percent for first-time marriages and 31 percent for all marriages—and has been declining for years.

# 3

# Happily Ever After

## Why Most Marriages
## Are Happy, Not Hard

Not long ago, before speaking at an event at a well-known private university, I asked for a quick meeting with the university executive who had arranged for me to come in. This man is a leader in higher education, plus he and his wife are very involved in the marriage arena and speak regularly at large marriage conferences.

I wanted to share the good news about marriage I was finding and get their feedback and input. So we sat in a student cafeteria for a few minutes, and I began outlining the five truths in this book that counter the different myths people believe about marriage. But when I got to the subject of this chapter, instead of simply telling them what I was seeing, I decided to demonstrate.

I said, "Wait a second and I'll show you something."

I walked over to two graduate students at the café table next to us and apologized for interrupting but explained that I was a social researcher and I had a random question for them: "What percentage of couples do you think are happy in their marriage today? Not perfect, but not just so-so roommates either. What percent do you think are happy?"

Both twenty-something women laughed a little bit, and one said, "I'd say about 30 to 40 percent" (which is about what I usually hear). The other one said, "No, I don't think it is that high. With everything we hear, I'd say more like 15 percent."

I told them, "Would you believe it is around 80 percent? Lots of surveys have found a little lower or little higher, but the average is probably around 80 percent."

They, of course, were stunned. And encouraged. "Wow! That is amazing." "That's really great to know, actually!"

I walked back over to the university executive and his wife and noticed that they looked surprised, even flustered. I sat back down across from them, and they just stared at me for a moment.

The husband finally said, "Wow."

The wife shook her head. "That was amazing. That really opened my eyes. And you made your point—very effectively, by the way!"

The husband said, "I'm having a hard time processing what I just saw and heard. This changes everything regarding how we should talk about marriage and divorce at our marriage conferences. We are so focused on emphasizing how marriage is in trouble to motivate people to not be one of the statistics. But I can see that it might demoralize them instead. And if most marriages are happy, that may mean that many of the couples at the conference are doing well and are there for inspiration or equipping because they want to *keep* doing well." He paused. "I'm really going to have to think about what this means."

## The Truth About Happiness in Marriage

I have seen that type of response more times than I can count from average people on the street and from those who work with married couples. Although I hear a variety of opinions, of course, most people think about one-third of couples are happy in their marriages. Even more telling, it is quite rare that someone will guess a number higher than 50 percent. For every twenty people I ask, I might hear two or three who believe happy couples are in the majority.

> Most married people today enjoy being married to their spouse and, given the chance, would do it all over again.

I certainly used to have the same impression, so I was stunned when I started to realize the truth was very different. It turns out most married people today enjoy being married to their spouse and, given the chance, would do it all over again. And the numbers are even better in certain demographic groups. Our research also found much good news even for those couples who, right now, are unhappy and struggling.

Let's look at three of these truths in more detail.

## Truth 1: Around 80 Percent of Marriages Are Happy

There are so many studies about marital satisfaction (including one of my own) that it was impossible for Tally and me to investigate them all. But as far as we can tell, they have all found similar things: the vast majority of couples are happy in their marriages. Yes, clearly, sometimes trouble comes, and when it does, the happiness numbers can change very quickly. But thankfully, for the majority, the ups and downs seem to mostly keep couples in an overall happy place.

To show you the overwhelming evidence for this, let me first describe my own study, and then I'll list several others.

### *My* Surprising Secrets of Highly Happy Marriages *Study*[41]

From 2010 to 2012 I extensively interviewed and surveyed married couples about their happiness in marriage and their various day-to-day habits for my book *The Surprising Secrets of Highly Happy Marriages*.

I was primarily interested in learning what the happiest couples did differently that was making them so happy and that others could replicate. This study included anonymous surveys of 1,304 married people—652 married couples—which were conducted either internally (by me and my team) or by the research firm Decision Analyst (with whom we have worked on all our nationally representative surveys), and which provided a confidence level of 95 percent, plus or minus 5 percent. To ensure that neither spouse knew what the other had said, the spouses were always separated for the survey.

I identified the happiest couples by having each spouse answer this question:

---

**Are you, personally, generally happy in your marriage these days and enjoying being married? (Choose one answer.)**

---

1. Yes!

2. Yes, most of the time.

3. It depends—sometimes yes, sometimes no.

4. Not really.

5. No! I am really unhappy.

---

The couples I wanted to study for *The Surprising Secrets of Highly Happy Marriages* were the ones where both the husband and the wife independently and anonymously answered "Yes!" But since I had the ability to analyze *couples,* not just survey *individuals,* I also wanted to learn what percentage of husbands and wives independently agreed that they were happy.

As you'll see below, most studies find an extraordinarily high percentage of survey takers (usually above 90 percent) saying that they are happy in their marriages, and researchers have understandably been skeptical of those percentages. After all, just because a husband or wife says "Yes, I'm happy" doesn't mean that their spouse would agree—which would mean the couple wouldn't be considered truly happy.

My survey, by contrast, was designed to weed out those

cases, since I was categorizing participants as couples, taking into account what each spouse said. We broke down the respondents into three categories. Here are the results from my internal surveys:[42]

### The Highly Happy couples—34 percent

These were what I call the Yes! couples, where both the husband and wife independently and anonymously answered that "Yes!" they were happy and enjoying marriage (answer choice 1). Any couple where either spouse picked an answer other than this was put into one of the categories below.

### The Happy couples—37 percent

These are couples where both partners answered that they were happy most of the time, or one answered "Yes!" and the other answered "Yes, most of the time."

### The So-So and Struggling couples—29 percent

Any couple where one or both spouses picked choices 3, 4, or 5 was put in this group. Most were in this group because one partner answered "Sometimes yes, sometimes no." There were many telling mismatches, where one partner said he or she was happy and the other party said "Sometimes" or "Not really" (such couples were always placed in this third group).

It was very encouraging that 71 percent of married couples were happy, with one-third being highly happy!

Even most of the 29 percent who aren't listed as happy have a "sometimes yes, sometimes no" marriage; in other words, the so-so relationship that most people seem to think is the majority. But it isn't! Truth be told, the real happiness ratio is probably even higher than 71 percent, since several of the venues in which we did these surveys were likely to attract couples with a greater need for marriage intervention.

You can find out more details on what I found in this study (including the very telling habits of the highly happy couples) in *The Surprising Secrets of Highly Happy Marriages* or at www .surprisingsecrets.com.

### What Percent of Marriages Are Happy, According to Other Studies?

Beyond my own research, the following pages list what other studies have found.

Looking at my poll and all the others, the median number of those who say they are in happy marriages is around 90 percent. Although these numbers are certainly encouraging, it is likely that most of these surveys asking about happiness or satisfaction don't tell the whole story.

First of all, the survey language is often vague and probably doesn't offer enough choice at the bottom end of the scale. But more important, my own survey found that there was a nine percentage point drop from the number of *individuals* who described

## Happiness Results from Other Studies*

| Study and Findings | Percent Happy or Very Happy |
|---|---|
| The General Social Survey (GSS) has been run by the National Opinion Research Center at the University of Chicago[43] since 1972. Their overall happiness numbers have remained fairly consistent over the last forty years, with around 98 percent of respondents describing their marriages as happy. These 2012 results are not yet published but were tabulated for us by GSS director Dr. Tom Smith:[44] | 98% |
| *Taking all things together, how would you describe your marriage?*<br>    Very happy—65.4%<br>    Pretty happy—32.2%<br>    Not too happy—2.3% | |
| A 2005 survey conducted by the Office of Survey Research at the University of Texas–Austin for the National Fatherhood Initiative Marriage Survey (NFIMS) found 96 percent described their marriage as happy, and 88 percent as "completely" or "very" satisfied with their marriage.[45] | 96% |
| *Taking things altogether, how would you describe your marriage?*<br>    Very happy—68.5%<br>    Pretty happy—27.9%<br>    Not too happy—3.6% | |
| *All in all, how satisfied are you with your marriage?*<br>    Completely satisfied—50%<br>    Very satisfied—38%<br>    Somewhat satisfied—9%<br>    Not very satisfied—2%<br>    Not at all satisfied—1% | |
| A GfK Roper poll (likely 2008) for Divorce360 .com found that most people described a happy marriage as one where the couple was happy at least three-quarters of the time and that 75 percent | 75% |

of respondents indeed described themselves that way.[46]

*Those who say they are happy in their marriages...*
At least three-quarters of the time—75%
At least half the time—15%
Never happy—5%[47]

| | |
|---|---|
| Marist conducted a 2010 poll for the Knights of Columbus,[48] finding the following happiness levels among those who are married:<br><br>Very happy—58%<br>Happy—33%<br>Not very happy—7%<br>Not happy at all—2% | 91% |
| Dr. Brad Wilcox with the National Marriage Project conducted a survey of married couples with children at home and ran a special analysis for me comparing the answers of husbands and wives to each other in the same categories as my *Surprising Secrets of Highly Happy Marriages* study. Even though these marriages are statistically more likely to be strained (by the child-rearing years), 72 percent were still happy![49]<br><br>Very happy—26%<br>Happy—46%<br>Less than happy—28% | 72% |
| Several state-specific studies have found similar results. One highly regarded 2001 study, "Marriage in Oklahoma," was conducted by an all-star group of researchers, including Dr. Scott Stanley, the senior program consultant for the project.[50] This study discovered over two-thirds of Oklahoma couples were very happy.<br><br>*Would you say your marriage is:*<br>Very happy—68%<br>Pretty happy—29%<br>Not too happy—3% | 97% |

*Due to rounding, some totals do not equal 100%.

their marriage as happy and the number of *couples* that actually were happy once you take both spouses' answers into account. I think the same scenario is likely to apply to the other studies of individuals. So applying a similar haircut would bring down the median happiness ratio for couples to around an 80 percent level.[51]

As I told the graduate students in the café that day, the actual percentage of happy marriages could be a bit lower or higher, but 80 percent seems like a very safe—in some ways, even conservative—number. And while the estimate may be conservative, the reactions to this good news are anything but. Consistently, when I share this statistic with an audience in a marriage seminar or women's conference, I usually lose the audience for a few moments as an excited buzz sweeps the room. One highly effective counselor told me,

> Someone once said the bulk of marriages end with a whimper not a bang. They just feel trapped and with no way out. So I do a lot of "What ifs" to get hurting couples to see a good option or explanation rather than a bad one. Like, "What if your husband wasn't intending to hurt you— what's another possible explanation for his action here?"
>
> Well, having heard the real happiness numbers, now I want to start saying, "What if the vast majority of marriages are in good shape? If that is true, then you are an outlier, not the norm—and if most other marriages are able to get to happiness, you can too. We can solve this and get you back to where you want to be!"

## Truth 2: Most People Are Glad They Married Their Spouse—and Would Do It All Over Again

Other surveys have gotten at the happiness question a different way, confirming some other good marriage news.

A Marist poll found that 95 percent of married individuals said they married the right person. The National Fatherhood Initiative Marriage Survey (NFIMS), mentioned earlier, found that 93 percent would marry their spouse all over again.[52] Only 13 percent of respondents had gone through a bad enough marriage patch to consider divorce. And most touching, 97 percent expected to be married for life. See the table below.

### So Glad We Did It...

**A Marist Poll, Published in August 2010[53]**

*Do you think you married the right person, or not?*
Yes—95%
No—5%

**The National Fatherhood Initiative Marriage Survey (NFIMS)[54]**

*Would you marry the same person if you had to do it over again?*
Yes—93%
No—7%

*Since you married (married your current spouse), have you ever seriously considered filing for divorce?*
Yes—13%
No—87%

*Do you expect to be married for life?*
Yes—97%
No—3%

## Truth 3: Most of Those Who Aren't Happy Will Be If They Stay Committed for Five Years

But what about those couples who aren't happy? There is good news for them too. The Institute for American Values published a scholarly report a few years back that analyzed several findings about happiness from the National Survey of Families and Households (NSFH). Led by *The Case for Marriage* author Linda Waite, and including several other highly regarded researchers, this report asked an important question with its title *Does Divorce Make People Happy?*

The answer to that question, it turns out, is largely no. The researchers were stunned to discover that the grass wasn't usually greener. Generally speaking, the unhappy adults who were perhaps trying to escape one type of pain by divorcing instead experienced a different type of pain. For instance, they showed an increase in signs of depression and alcohol use compared to those unhappy couples who stayed married.[55] Many divorce lawyers I have interviewed tell me that this rings true for them. Not long after a divorce, their clients are often surprised by just how little time they really have with their kids or how much trouble is being caused by the split itself, not just the conflict that led to it. Several years down the road, some clients privately say, "If I had known, I might not have done it."

Thankfully, according to the above study, if an unhappy couple *does* stick with their marriage, the vast majority are happy within five years, with the largest improvement coming for those who were the most miserable. Two conclusions from the report:[56]

- "Two out of three unhappily married adults who avoided divorce or separation ended up happily married five years later."[57]
- "Among those who rated their marriages as very unhappy, almost eight out of ten who avoided divorce were happily married five years later."[58]

And this is not an isolated finding; the Oklahoma study mentioned earlier corroborates that people are grateful they didn't give up on a troubled marriage. Among those whose marriages had been in enough trouble to consider divorce, the vast majority said they were glad they had stuck it out and were still together (79 percent of those married seven years or less, rising to 95 percent or more after the first seven years of marriage).[59]

Several psychologists, therapists, and other counselors who had already been aware of these studies, especially the likelihood of being happy within five years, have told me that this one piece of good news alone is life changing for many couples. Because what often causes someone to actually throw in the towel is simply not being able to see when the pain will end.

A few years ago, Jeff and I watched a few seasons of the Discovery Channel reality show *Out of the Wild,* in which a group of average people are dropped into a vast, harsh, and very remote wilderness environment (for example, Alaska) and must find their way to civilization. They are given no food, water, or shelter (they have to find and build it all) and—most important—no map to where or how far away civilization is. But they *are* given a handset with a big tempting button that they can press to be rescued if they just can't take it anymore.

It turns out that what torpedoes most of the participants is not the grinding hunger or the agony of blistered feet or the freezing nights—it is the open-endedness of the pain. It is not knowing how long it will be until things get better. Most could clearly last it out if they knew *I only have three more days to go,* but they don't know whether it will be three days or three months. So when they are at their lowest, they push the Eject button.

It works the same way in marriage. Imagine the difference for hurting couples to know *Yes, we've been miserable for a few years, but most couples in our situation are actively* happy *within five years, so we can stick it out that long and work to get better.*

## An Opportunity for Those Who Lead

Like many in the general public, countless leaders I've talked to assume most marriages are in the so-so category. But I also interviewed several priests, pastors, and leaders of marriage-related nonprofits who knew the truth, either from specific research or simply because, as one put it, the more negative numbers "just didn't pass the smell test."

And as a result, in many cases these leaders had changed their programming or the big-picture strategy of how they worked with marriages. Listen in on one pastor's comments:

Well, I've heard that most couples are just getting by, but at least here we are seeing something different. We did a survey of our congregation, and 86 percent of the married folks said they liked being married and didn't really get much out of the stuff we were doing for hurting couples. Mostly, we realized folks needed encouragement and supportive fellowship, with a little bit of equipping.

So we redesigned our marriage ministry to focus more on fun things for the couple and ways to catch problems before they start. For example, we provide childcare on Friday nights once a month so couples can go on date nights. We have even gotten the nearby restaurants and theater to sponsor some date nights.

Twice a year we do a big Friday night event to bring everyone together, and we use that to funnel people into couples' small groups. We train the small-group leaders to spot trouble early. The whole process is designed to generate community, so if a couple starts to have trouble, someone will clue in.

We've always had an active group of marriage counselors. But by the time you decide to go to a counselor, you're probably pretty unhappy. We realized we needed a way to support the folks who were happy and wanted to stay that way.

Similar to this pastor, several leaders of churches and other membership organizations mentioned doing a survey to discover what the needs actually are and then developing a ministry model to meet them. FamilyLife has been offering its Family Needs Survey to congregations for years, and you'll see some of the aggregate (anonymous) results of what they've learned in these pages. (If you're interested in exploring a Family Needs Survey, the website is www.familylife.com/FNS.) We will highlight other options on our website www.goodnewsmarriage.com over time.

Beyond that, if you are a leader looking for different models of marriage ministry, go to our website to see the piece entitled "Three Sample Models of Marriage Ministry," featuring three short interviews with leaders who have developed different ways of doing marriage ministry within a church, each of which is working well for many different congregations.

## But Should We Be Focusing on Happiness in Marriage?

Although the secret longing for a happy, lifelong marriage is one of the deepest desires of the human heart, many people these days understandably worry about focusing on marital happiness.

We have all seen the terrible difficulties that come when someone looks to marriage or their spouse to make them happy— when someone expects an imperfect person to deliver what I believe only God can deliver. We have all seen the tragic outcome of what happens when someone concludes *I'm not happy, so I'm out of here.*

As a result many of us who work with marriages have focused

more on saying that marriage is about serving the other person—that we need to plan to endure times of tribulation, work hard, and not expect a primrose path.

And all of that is true. But when that is *all* we share about marriage, we and everyone else begin to assume that most marriages aren't happy. It is so easy to discourage people about marriage without intending to! *If it's not going to be the abundant, joyful, delightful union my heart is longing for,* the average young person might think, *and if getting married doesn't make my companionship with this other person better, why bother getting married?* One well-respected marriage and family pastor discussed it with me this way:

> Gary Thomas's book *Sacred Marriage* is one of my top two favorite marriage books. That subtitle is amazing: *What If God Designed Marriage to Make Us Holy More Than to Make Us Happy?* And I see how God uses my own marriage to teach me the truth of unconditional love.
>
> But I think the problem in the church is that we've also developed this tone that marriage is a bit of a beatdown and by God's design it is supposed to be a bit brutal. Paul says that those who marry will have trouble. We need to preach that, but we shouldn't say, "Marriage will teach you to endure," without also highlighting things like Proverbs 5:18, "Rejoice in the wife of your youth"!

We need to say that God's ultimate design is that I'm supposed to enjoy marriage with my wife and walk through this life with her! That is just as much in the Bible. Gary Thomas is right about countering romanticism, but I wonder if now the pendulum has swung too much the other way. We need to hold out the need to work on your marriage, without saying that God is trying to make you miserable with marriage!

> "We need to say that God's ultimate design is that I'm supposed to enjoy marriage with my wife and walk through this life with her!"

A few years back, Jeff and I were doing a weekend marriage conference for a ministry outside of Boston. We mentioned how easy it is to fall into a pattern of saying "Marriage is hard" even though, despite the inevitable challenges, most people would not actually describe their marriage that way. What seems much more universal and accurate, we shared, is that we sometimes have to *work* hard in our marriages.

The worship leader and Christian singer at that event was Danny Oertli, and as we were saying this, I happened to look over to where he and his wife were sitting and noticed that his mind looked a hundred miles away.

The next week he e-mailed us, "Something in your talk inspired me. To be honest, once I heard you guys say it, I zoned out and went into 'songwriter world.' You were talking about how people always say marriage is so hard, when it often really isn't. We totally relate! So here's a super-rough version of a song I wrote yesterday and scratched out late last night."

Jeff and I listened to his song together, and when we got to the chorus, we had tears in our eyes. Here are just the opening lyrics. (You can hear the whole rough cut of the song at our website for this book, www.goodnewsmarriage.com, but I'm hoping Danny officially records it at some point!)

**It's So Hard**
(unpublished song by Danny Oertli)[60]

I can still remember what the preacher said, when we
    were at the altar hand in hand.
All his words were filled with gloom and dread, about
    how hard a marriage is, harder than you think.
Well I'm glad I didn't turn and run that night. Because all
    these years later, I guess he did get one thing right.

[Chorus]

It's so hard to leave you in the morning,
It's so hard not to think of you all day,
And it's so hard just waiting for your loving.
And I agree with what that preacher said: it's so hard.

It is so vital for us to affirm that although there *are* many marriages that are hard or go through hard times, that most of the time, marriage is delightful—that it's okay to hope and work for that type of marriage, even as we emphasize that *not* having it is never an excuse to give up.

Because the good-news truth is that in most cases marriage is the most amazing, delightful, and profound earthly relationship that any of us will ever know. The truth is that although most couples have to work at marriage, and some will go through very hard times, most come out the other side and enjoy each other for a lifetime. The truth is that although we can never look to marriage to *make* us happy, we need to be trumpeting the fact that when a couple chooses wisely and then takes the scary but wonderful step of commitment for life, they are much more likely to have that abundant relationship they are hoping for.

## Summary

- Most people erroneously assume that most marriages aren't particularly happy, which is very demoralizing.
- Many people are cynical about marriage—or avoid it entirely—as a result.
- In reality, though, around 80 percent of marriages are happy, with around 30 percent being very happy!
- The vast majority (93 percent or more) are glad they married their spouse and would do it all over

again—including those who had at one time considered divorce.

- Most of those who are the least happy will be the most happy if they stay committed for five years.
- Marriage may require hard work, but that doesn't mean that most marriages are hard. For most couples, marriage is the most delightful earthly relationship that they will ever know.

## Good News #2

The vast majority of marriages are happy (around 80 percent)! Most people are glad they married their spouse and, given the chance, would do it all over again.

# 4

# We Gather Together

## How Active Faith Lowers the Divorce Rate

F ew things are more unsettling than working hard, trying to do the right things, and getting no more benefit than someone who does all the wrong things and doesn't care. Similarly, few things are more demoralizing than working hard to teach *others* to do the right things and seeing the same dynamic unfold.

Thankfully, doing the right things usually leads to a payoff. Eating right keeps you healthier than those who don't, and teaching a child to study hard usually earns him higher grades.

But those in the faith community have become disheartened by the idea that this same principle doesn't seem to apply to marriage. Pastors and priests have worked so hard to support couples through premarital counseling, teaching the important precepts that the Bible says will protect marriages, and counseling those with troubled marriages. Many churchgoers have tried hard to follow biblical marriage principles about selflessness, love, respect, forgiveness, and keeping no record of wrongs, even when it is difficult.

And yet we hear it doesn't make any difference. For more than a decade, it has been common to hear that the rate of divorce in the church is the same as the rate in the culture at large. And since the popular belief is that half of all marriages end in divorce, most churchgoers and pastors then think, *Half of all marriages among these people here, sitting in this church, despite all this work, will end in divorce.*

A friend of mine who is working through tough issues in her marriage says that thought quickly becomes personal: she looks around her church and thinks, *If half of these people are getting divorced, what chance do I have?*

As we listen to the depressing statistics, those initial thoughts can lead to others, some of which are so subconscious that we don't even say them out loud: *If what we hear is true, all my hard work—as a pastor, leader, counselor, or congregant—means nothing. If this is true, how can I really encourage a young couple to worship together if it makes no difference?* Or even: *If this is true…if following the Bible has no impact on something as vitally important as marriage…what does that say about the Bible?*

Well, thankfully, we can stop thinking those depressing thoughts…because they aren't true!

## The Truth Is Encouraging

A few years ago, my husband, Jeff, and I were in an elevator at a convention of ministry leaders, and we were discussing that morning's media story on new divorce data that again gave the wrong impression about a 50 percent divorce rate.[61] I said something about the first-marriage divorce rate being closer to 25 percent and that it is significantly lower in the church—and heard a gasp from the woman behind us.

We turned, and she introduced herself, sharing that she owned one of the few Christian bookstores in the area. She said, "I'm sorry...I couldn't help overhearing your conversation. Could you explain what you just said?"

As we walked toward the convention hall, she listened with a stunned look on her face as I gave her a brief rundown on my research. She said, "I wish you could have arrived in time to share this with the keynote speakers before they spoke yesterday. A major part of their talk was about how all these social problems are the same in the church—including the 50 percent divorce rate. I looked around at four thousand people in this giant ballroom and saw everyone's shoulders just slump. It was so discouraging. I'm sure the speakers wanted to encourage us to work harder to help marriages in the church. But they don't understand how disempowering that 'fact' has been for those of us who already do try to help marriages. It is insidious. What a huge thing that it isn't true!"

Thankfully, what we hear *isn't* true. Not even close! Every study that has ever been done has found that the rate of divorce among those who regularly attend church is much lower than among those who don't. I'll explain the research shortly, but the bottom line is that weekly church attendance alone lowers the divorce rate significantly—roughly 25 to 50 percent, depending on the study and group of people being studied.[62]

> Weekly church attendance alone lowers the divorce rate significantly—roughly 25 to 50 percent, depending on the study.

The popular belief that the rate of divorce is the same inside and outside the church is based on a deeply entrenched *misunderstanding* about the results of several George Barna surveys over the past decades. A misunderstanding that, Mr. Barna told me, he would love to correct in the public's mind.

So let me briefly explain how this confusion arose and outline the true facts from several different, representative studies, including my new analysis of previously unpublished Barna data.

## Myth Based on a Misunderstanding

For years, George Barna and the Barna Group have been at the forefront of research into beliefs and practices in faith and culture. In 2001, Barna released a widely quoted study that showed that professing Christians had the same divorce rate as non-Christians—roughly 33 to 34 percent.

The news media understandably jumped on it. The original Barna study came out not long after the resurgence of the conservative movement and the growth in evangelical churches had put family values front and center. So the finding that professing Christians had the same divorce rate as everyone else was a black eye for the church. Pastors everywhere were shocked and began talking about this sobering reality from the pulpit, exhorting followers of Jesus that they shouldn't look like the culture at large and that those who believe marriage is a covenant before God should instead be those who take their marriage vows most seriously.

While the instruction to Christians to take marriage seriously is a great message, the desperation behind it was unfounded. Unfortunately, at this point two major misunderstandings had become entwined and taken on a life of their own: First, the idea that the current divorce rate was 50 percent, which as you now know, it isn't. And second, the idea that the divorce rate is the same "in the church," which you'll soon see isn't accurate either.

A Barna specialty is digging deep into people's beliefs and how their beliefs and actions change over time in this modern culture. But what many clergy, marriage leaders, and news reporters didn't realize was that this particular Barna study was designed to dig out divorce trends based on faith-based *beliefs* and was not designed to look at faith-based *practices* such as going to church. Simply stated, the Barna researchers were studying those who professed to hold Christian beliefs, not those who went to church. In fact, in keeping with the adage that "Going to church doesn't make you a Christian any more than sitting in a garage makes you a car," Barna specifically *excluded* church attendance from the analysis. They did ask whether the survey takers had been to worship services in the last week, the last month, and so on, but that factor was not included in the analysis.

But most people didn't realize that. As the years passed and other Barna studies continued to show the same trend, it became firmly entrenched in the churchgoing public mind that *Barna finds that the rate of divorce is the same in the church as it is in the world.* And at the same time, because of the myth that half of all marriages end in divorce, this translated to the inaccurate conclusion that *just like in the overall population, half of all marriages in the church end in divorce.*

As I have interviewed and surveyed hundreds of pastors, ministry leaders, marriage mentors, and others, it is clear that is what many leaders believe as well.

The first time I spoke about this topic publicly was at a 2012 conference for marriage and family pastors and other leaders, and I was delighted to see that George Barna was one of the other speakers. In the speaker break room ahead of time, I explained to Mr. Barna what I was going to be sharing and asked for his thoughts about how widespread this misunderstanding has become.

He said he was glad I was bringing light to this because, as he put it, "The wrong information spreads so quickly today. Someone puts a number out on the Internet and says some study found this, and everyone believes it. That happens to us all the time. Many times I'll be driving down the street listening to someone on the radio say, 'As George Barna found...' and it will be something I've never even studied."

I thanked him for his encouragement, went onstage to tell these pastors what I'm telling you in this book—and realized just how many faith leaders today *need* this encouragement! That first talk was embarrassingly unpolished, with thirty minutes of solid data, not nearly enough helpful stories, and PowerPoint slides that weren't pretty at all…and yet I was stunned to see many of the pastors standing up to take pictures of the slides on their cell phones.

So in the interest of countering the "wrong information," as Mr. Barna put it, what is the truth?

## Getting a Handle on Truth

There are many distinctive and credible studies about the impact of religiosity, and I found it easy to get confused by differences in the results. Even a small variation in the objective or hypothesis—for example, a study of "religious affiliation" versus "religious practices"—can yield quite diverse results.[63]

I don't want to get lost in the technicalities, so the bottom line is this: numerous well-known sociologists, demographers, psychologists, and other researchers have found that when someone is active in their faith, it lowers their chances of divorce—usually significantly. These experts, many of whom have taken the time to personally correspond or meet with us about their research, include Brad Wilcox, Annette Mahoney, Steve Beach (along with Frank Fincham), Chris Ellison, Tim Heaton, and Scott Stanley. (Since it is difficult to analyze the sincerity of an individual's faith, most of these researchers studied actions such as regular worship attendance as a signal of how much the person prioritized and lived out their faith.) Although there are fewer major nationwide surveys looking at this today compared to years past, those that have (including several conducted by those named above) have found the same trend as before.

There are, in fact, so many studies it would be easy to get overwhelmed. So in this chapter, we present only the four studies we view as most significant. (Others are discussed in the FAQ section at the end of the book.)

### Study 1: Barna Group[64]—Divorce Rate Drops 27 Percent Among Churchgoers

Barna Group has been a great partner as I have tried to understand the relationship between being a churchgoer and divorce. I commissioned them to run a tabulation on several of their most recent data sets, with one new factor included: Did the person go to church last week? In 2008 (the last year they published a study publicly) among professing Christians who had *also* been in church in the last seven days, the divorce rate dropped 27 percent compared to those who hadn't.[65] As you can see in the table below, an average of 33 percent of adult survey takers nationwide had ever been divorced. But among Christians who had attended church in the last seven days, the divorce rate was 27 percent. Among everyone else, it was 37 percent. Among Catholics and evangelicals, the numbers were even more positive.

### The Impact of Church Attendance on Divorce Rate

|  | Ever divorced | Never divorced |
|---|---|---|
| US population (in general) | 33% | 67% |
| Christians who attended church in the last 7 days | 27% | 73% |
| Everyone else (non-Christian, not in church last 7 days) | 37% | 63% |
| **Subgroups** | | |
| Evangelical weekly attenders[66] | 25% | 75% |
| Catholic weekly attenders | 22% | 78% |

Source: Barna Group, 2008 OmniPoll (special analysis for Shaunti Feldhahn).

As you can see, being part of a church community does make a difference. That is good news![67] It is also encouraging to know that the impact found by the Barna Group is on the *low* end of the scale. Other studies have found an even bigger improvement in the divorce rate among churchgoers—mostly due to the impact of church attendance itself, rather than other factors. The next study is a great example.

### Study 2: Brad Wilcox and the "Cultural Contradictions" Study[68]—Divorce Rate Drops by 50 Percent Among Churchgoers, and Most of That Is Due to Church Attendance, Not Other Factors

The landmark National Survey of Families and Households (NSFH) is one of the largest, most detailed, and precise surveys to address the topics of religion and divorce[69] and has been used by many social scientists. Based at the University of Wisconsin Center of Demography and Ecology and led by Dr. Larry Bumpass and Dr. James Sweet, the survey conducted three separate waves of interviews with thirteen thousand people between 1987 and 1994.[70]

A major study on this data by Dr. Brad Wilcox found that regular attendance (several times a month) had a major impact on reducing divorce rates. In "The Cultural Contradictions of Mainline Family Ideology and Practice," Wilcox documents that those who attend worship services regularly have an average drop of roughly 50 percent in their divorce rates compared to those who do not.[71]

Further, Dr. Wilcox found that most of the reduction in divorce among churchgoers can be conclusively tied to the impact of church attendance itself and not some of the other factors that come along with it. For example, churchgoers tend to be more educated and well off, but since those factors also lower the risk of divorce, Dr. Wilcox wanted to find whether it was church attendance or those socioeconomic factors that were more important.

He discovered that even after controlling for many other factors, such as income, age, gender, race, ethnicity, education, and geographic region, the matter of church attendance trumped them all. Church attendance alone decreases the divorce rate substantially. Among mainline Protestants, for example, church attendance alone dropped the divorce rate 35 percent even after other factors are eliminated.[72] See the table below.

## Reduction in Divorce for Active Churchgoers*

|  | Actual Reduction in Divorce Rate | Reduction in Divorce Rate Attributed to Church Attendance Alone** |
|---|---|---|
| Overall Average[73] | 50% | 35% |
| Active Mainline Protestant | 54% | 35% |
| Active Conservative Protestant[74] | 44% | 35% |
| Active Catholic | 50% | 31% |

*As compared to those who do not regularly attend church. "Active" is defined as attending several times per month.

**After controlling for socioeconomic factors.

## Study 3: Religious Influences and Divorce[75]—a Couple Who Shares the Same Faith and Attends Services Together Regularly Is 35 to 50 Percent Less Likely to Divorce Than Anyone Else

This study looked at divorce rates in a slightly different way yet yielded similar results. "Religious Influences on the Risk of Marital Dissolution" examined several religious aspects from a sample of almost three thousand couples married for the first time. Three leading sociologists looked closely at whether and how frequently partners attended religious services (church, synagogue, and so on), and whether they remained married or broke up during the five-year period between wave 1 and wave 2 of the NSFH (the very detailed survey mentioned earlier). An e-mail from lead author Dr. Christopher Ellison summarizes the results of the study:

Same-faith unions in which both partners attend services regularly are much less likely to dissolve over our five-year study period than virtually every other type of union. Specifically, they have 35 to 50 percent lower odds of dissolution than same-faith unions with less frequent attendance, or mixed-faith unions regardless of attendance pattern. (This latter category includes unions that involve non-religious partners.) These apparent religious differences withstand statistical controls for socio-demographic factors, marital duration, and multiple measures of baseline marital quality—in other words, these are "net" religious differences among couples who are generally similar on this broad array of other characteristics.[76]

Simply stated, couples who go to church or other religious services together on a regular basis have the lowest divorce rate of any group studied, regardless of other factors such as how long they've been married. For example, they have better odds than two professing Christians who do not attend church regularly or a couple where one spouse attends regularly and one does not.

### Study 4: FamilyLife Family Needs Survey, 2012–2013[77]—Among More Than Fifty Churches Surveyed, Total Divorce Rate (Including Second and Third Marriages) Was Only 22 Percent

Over the course of multiple years, the large ministry FamilyLife has been surveying those in congregations so pastors and staff can get valuable feedback on what is working and what areas of family ministry may need the most attention.

In the 2012–2013 survey among 6,171 ever-married persons in more than fifty churches, only 22.4 percent have ever been divorced. (And that divorce rate is almost certainly overstated because the survey captured baby boomers at much higher rates—and the baby boomer generation has by far the highest rates of divorce. A church survey that included a more representative sample of younger age groups would almost certainly find an average churchgoer divorce rate of under 20 percent.)[78] You can find a summary of this survey at www.familylife.com/FNS.

## The Power of Prayer and Other Religious Activities

Several other studies provide a window into the impact of religious actions beyond church attendance—factors such as praying or reading the Bible.

Before I get to what we do know so far, let me mention what we don't. I have heard several marriage counselors, pastors, or other leaders say things like "Those who pray together have only a 5 percent divorce rate" or "Those who regularly meet together with others outside of church have a 1 percent divorce rate." I have seen that type of statistic printed in quite a few articles and books. However, Tally and I have been unable to substantiate those ultra-low divorce numbers, and they appear to be based more on myth than reality.

One number in particular spread widely due to a Dr. Phil book, *Relationship Rescue,* which quotes a Christian discipleship series by David McLaughlin that supposedly says the divorce rate among married spouses that pray together is one in ten thousand. However, we listened to every one of the long audios of that series and did not hear McLaughlin say that statistic anywhere.[79] Because we have not been able to trace McLaughlin himself, and because Dr. Phil's representatives have not been able to provide any information, we are forced to conclude, for now, anyway, that that particular number is more myth than fact.

We have also seen a misunderstanding of the conclusions cited in the book *Faithful Attraction* by iconic and sometimes controversial Catholic sociologist Andrew Greeley. Greeley calculated a 1 percent "possibility of divorce" when couples prayed together and had a highly satisfying sexual relationship with their spouse. He describes this finding as based on two surveys run by Gallup Poll, originally for *Psychology Today,* back in 1989–90, along with his own analysis of the General Social Survey (one of the surveys referenced in chapter 2). Gallup has not been able to provide us this particular Gallup Poll from the pre-digital age so we cannot examine the study or confirm the book's data calculations. And even assuming the poll exists, what Greeley means by "possibility of divorce" is whether the couple *thinks* they might divorce, which is a very different thing from their actual divorce rate.

In both these cases, since we have eight years of experience in seeing that we have to eyeball *the actual study* in order to find out whether it truly says such and such or not, we simply have no way of knowing if those ultra-low divorce numbers actually exist. And for now it appears that they do not. (But if you are aware of concrete research we have missed, please contact us through our website.)

Although we haven't yet seen actual studies linking the impact of prayer (or other actions of faith) to much lower divorce rates, it wouldn't surprise me if a more direct correlation between prayer and low divorce rates is found by researchers in the future. What we *do* know about prayer so far is that couples who pray have much healthier and more connected marriages than those who don't, which should, theoretically, improve the chance of the marriage lasting for a lifetime.

I'm including three relevant studies below. (We reference several others in the FAQ section.)

### Study 1: My *Surprising Secrets of Highly Happy Marriages* Study / Wilcox Data[80]—Those Who Are Active in Their Faith Are the Happiest in Their Marriages

Faith-related actions (like worship attendance and being in a supportive community) appear to have a dramatic impact on the strength and happiness of a marriage. While the majority of both religious and non-religious couples are happy, those who are active in their faith are far more likely to be very happy.

Several times we have mentioned Dr. Brad Wilcox, director of the National Marriage Project. Each year, he and the Center for Marriage and Families produce a report on marriage entitled *The State of Our Unions,* and he ran a special analysis on the 2011 report data for my book *The Surprising Secrets of Highly Happy Marriages.* We found that couples in which both partners agree that "God is at the center of our marriage" are twice as likely to be at the highest level of happiness in marriage compared with those who do not share that type of faith commitment.

In fact, when both spouses said "God is at the center," fully 53 percent of those couples were at the highest possible level of marital happiness. That's huge! (See graph, next page.) Think about the implications: in a vibrant church with couples who are trying to put God first, *more than half* of them are not just "happy," they are at the highest level of marital happiness and enjoyment.

> In a vibrant church with couples who are trying to put God first, *more than half* of them are not just "happy," they are at the highest level of marital happiness and enjoyment.

As a different example, the Oklahoma survey mentioned in the happiness results in chapter 3 specifically examined the impact of church attendance on happiness. The total of those who said they were very happy was 72 percent among those who regularly attended worship services, twenty percentage points higher than those who never attended![81] An active faith and being a part of a supportive faith community tend to lead people into much higher levels of marital satisfaction.

In other words, if all this is true, not only are most marriages happy but most marriages of people in the average local church are very happy. What an encouraging finding for the average pastor or church counselor who is wondering if his or her work even makes a difference!

**Happiness Levels Among Couples
Where Both Spouses Agree
"God Is at the Center of Our Marriage"**

Note: to be categorized as "Very Happy" both the husband and wife had to independently declare that they were at the highest level of happiness in their marriage.

Source: *The Surprising Secrets of Highly Happy Marriages* study, Shaunti Feldhahn, 2013.

## Study 2: PREPARE/ENRICH Study by Dr. David Olson[82]—the Better the Couples' Agreement on Actions Such as Bible Reading and Prayer, the Closer and Happier the Couple Was

Dr. David Olson, professor emeritus at the University of Minnesota and founder of the highly respected assessment organization PREPARE/ENRICH, has surveyed over fifty thousand couples through the organization's relationship inventory assessment. The number of studies, articles, and books borne out of this research remains unparalleled in the marriage arena, including on how spiritual beliefs impact marriages, and Dr. Olson himself has been very helpful to us as we have done our research.

In the study "Spiritual Beliefs and Marriage," coauthored with Peter Larson, Olson examined various religious activities (like Bible reading and prayer) to measure and evaluate how much couples agreed with each other spiritually. In all twelve dimensions of the evaluation, the more couples agreed with each other on personal spiritual beliefs and practices, the better were their scores in areas such as marital satisfaction, conflict resolution, and couple closeness. For example, those who had a high spiritual agreement scored a 71 on the couple closeness scale, almost double the score of those marriages that experienced a low spiritual agreement (they scored 39).

### Study 3: Marriage Oneness Assessment—Couples Who Pray Together Are Likely to Be Connected and Close in Their Marriage, Whereas Those Who Don't Are Much More Likely to Be Disconnected

As a part of an eight-week small-group FamilyLife DVD study called *Marriage Oneness,*[83] 3,850 couples took a marriage assessment called the "Marriage Oneness Profile," administered online by PREPARE/ENRICH. Based on the couples' answers to the assessment tool, PREPARE/ENRICH ranks couples by how close and connected the marriage is.[84]

This survey found a link between frequency of prayer and how connected spouses are. Fully 68 percent of highly connected couples agreed or strongly agreed that they pray together regularly. Only 19 percent of highly connected couples reported not praying together regularly. By comparison, most highly disconnected couples (73 percent) reported no regular prayer with their spouse. Among those taking this assessment, it was unusual for a couple who prays together to feel highly disconnected in their overall relationship. (See table below.)

Note that this assessment was probably offered primarily through churches and taken primarily by churchgoers, and thus these percentages are not necessarily the same as what we would see in the general population. However, the bottom line that prayer is highly associated with connectedness is very likely to be the same.

### "My Partner and I Pray Together on a Regular Basis"

| Couple Connectedness | Strongly Disagree | Disagree | Undecided | Agree | Strongly Agree |
|---|---|---|---|---|---|
| Highly Connected (18%) | 5% | 14% | 16% | 26% | 42% |
| Connected (15%) | 8% | 16% | 15% | 19% | 20% |
| Committed (17%) | 14% | 18% | 16% | 18% | 14% |
| Disconnected (24%) | 24% | 27% | 25% | 23% | 18% |
| Highly Disconnected (26%) | 48% | 25% | 27% | 15% | 6% |

Source: "Marriage Oneness" surveys, tabulated by PREPARE/ENRICH for FamilyLife. Due to rounding, columns may not total 100%.

### "Keep On Rolling"

In addition to the speaking engagements I do for corporations, community groups, and other events, I speak at thirty or forty churches a year. For the last few years, I have often asked the senior pastor and/or the marriage pastor of those churches if I can brief them on the good news I have been finding. Universally they are encouraged…and sometimes chagrined. The pastor of one large church told me, "I have quoted every one of those bad statistics you just mentioned."

"I have too," I said. "I think most of us have."

"I think as pastors, we sometimes feel like we have to create a crisis of awareness to draw attention to something," he continued. "Just a few weeks ago when we started this current marriage series, I asked people, 'Think right now of your friends having trouble in their marriage. They need this upcoming message. Look around you… Half of us are struggling. We have to take this seriously.'" He paused for a minute. "We try very hard here to instill hope in every other area, but in talking about marriages, we are putting a seed of doubt into people. And that isn't something we should be doing. Hope is what you want to give as a leader. We say God is a redeemer. He takes what is broken, fallen, and seems unfixable and makes all things new."

"What difference will it make to you, knowing the real data?" I asked him.

"Well, I can't use my old stats, that's for sure!" He laughed.

"But more than that, we own up to things here, and I think I will want to own up to this one—to tell the congregation we were wrong and didn't realize it. We would actually say, 'This may have had a negative effect on you or discouraged you, and we're sorry. Because the truth is better than fiction. Even if your marriage isn't in a happy place, realize happy doesn't mean perfect. Happy means you put the marriage in front of the issue, and the commitment overrides everything.'"

As I have spoken with other pastors, I have often heard relief as well. One pastor who has seen marriages in his church thriving in recent years put it this way:

> I think to some degree pastors feel like *I need to preach a special marriage sermon every three months, and if I'm not, I am not doing my job.* But this data confirms what I have seen: that pastors don't have to preach "marriage" sermons all the time. We *do* need to be intentional as leaders to ensure our church is supporting marriages and is bringing couples together in community. But that doesn't mean we have to cover the main marriage scriptures every week from the pulpit. Instead, we can keep emphasizing that ultimately it is about just living out these "one anothers" of the Bible, just being a disciple. That is the *best* thing you can do for your marriage. The key for us is to keep on rolling, keep on showing our people how to be fully obedient followers.

Another pastor summed the sense of relief up well, saying,

I have long wanted to tell people, "Bring your friends to church; you'll get support for your marriage here." But I kept stopping myself because if we have the same divorce rate as everyone else, how can I make that claim? Hearing this is freedom. Freedom to say that not only can you believe in marriage, but you can believe in *Christian* marriage. It is freedom to say that the Bible *does* work, that what God says *does* make a difference. It is freedom to say what most of us have felt but second-guessed before: married people need a supportive community, and the church is the best place to get it.

## Summary

- The notion that "the divorce rate is the same in the church as in the general public" is not true. That is a fundamental misunderstanding of Barna Group data.
- In the study that is misquoted, Barna was researching the divorce trends based on faith-based *beliefs,* not faith-based *practices* like worship attendance, and in fact actually excluded consideration of whether the person went to religious services.

- New tabulations of the Barna data that include church attendance, as well as the findings of several other studies, show that when a person attends church, it lowers their chances of divorce by roughly 25 to 50 percent compared to those who do not attend.

- A special run of Brad Wilcox / National Marriage Project survey data for *The Surprising Secrets of Highly Happy Marriages* book found that among couples where both the husband and the wife agreed that "God is at the center of our marriage," fully 53 percent were at the highest possible level of marital happiness!

- A FamilyLife survey of more than fifty churches found an average overall divorce rate in those churches of 22.4 percent, and because this survey had a higher-than-normal sample of high-risk baby boomers, the actual average divorce rate for church-goers is likely to be lower.

- A FamilyLife and PREPARE/ENRICH assessment of 7,700 married people found that 68 percent of highly connected couples said they prayed together regularly and that 73 percent of highly disconnected couples said they didn't.

## Good News #3

The rate of divorce in the church is 25 to 50 percent lower than among those who don't attend worship services, and those who prioritize their faith and/or pray together are dramatically happier and more connected.

# 5

# Second-Chance Satisfaction

## Why Remarriages Are Much More Successful Than You Thought

I n my interviews for *The Surprising Secrets of Highly Happy Marriages,* when I spoke to those in a second marriage, I often heard comments like this woman's: "I know we've got an uphill battle. Sixty percent of second marriages fail, and we are both determined we're not going to be in that group."

Or these comments, from a couple explaining their very difficult first few years in what was a second marriage for both of them:

Her: We are very excited that we've defied the odds.
One of the reasons is that we intentionally chose
not to have children together because we learned
that having a child together would have brought
a harder dynamic. We wanted to feel that all three
of the children were our children.

Him: Also, we went into the relationship with the right expectations, knowing that it was going to be a struggle. We understood that it would be hard, so we were resolved to do whatever it took to make it as easy as possible on each other.

Her: There were times we thought we weren't going to make it and were going to be one of the statistics. But we had promised our commitment before God, and we are both stubborn and don't like to quit. There were plenty of times where if we'd lacked determination, it would have been so easy to throw in the towel. But believing that God can redeem anything, we had a vision of what it could be like if we chose to press on. And that gave us hope, although sometimes it was literally the last thread we were holding on to.

As I spoke to those who were in highly happy second marriages, it was wonderful to see this type of commitment and determination. But I was struck by how commonly I heard these couples talk about "the incredibly high failure rate of second and third marriages," which is popularly believed to be at least 60 percent and 73 percent, respectively.

I couldn't help being concerned, especially since I suspected that (as with all the other divorce numbers) those ratios might not be the full story. After all, if the feeling of futility adds pressure in first marriages, which are believed to have a "flip a coin" 50 percent failure rate, it must be smothering for those in second and third marriages to feel they are so *un*likely to succeed! For every couple that was motivated and determined by the statistics (such as the ones I was interviewing), how many were discouraged?

Although eight in ten marriages that exist today are first marriages (among women), it is still painful to think about the others, about those in a second or third marriage who believe that they have a better chance of winning at roulette than of keeping their marriage intact.

### What Percent of Marriages Are Remarriages?*

| | |
|---|---|
| First marriage | 80.5% |
| Second marriage | 15.8% |
| Third marriage (or more) | 3.8% |

*Among women. (Remarriage is more common among women, in part because women tend to live longer than men.) Source: US Census Bureau, SIPP table 10, 2009.

## Fueling the Legend

Because there are far fewer studies on remarriage in general, it is hard to get a handle on the right divorce statistics for those marriages—which is probably one reason why the wrong ones get so much traction. It appears that remarriages do face a moderately higher divorce rate (more on that below), but the ultra-high rates commonly cited and spread via the Internet appear, as far as we can tell after years of research, to be pure urban legend.

> The ultra-high rates commonly cited and spread via the Internet appear, as far as we can tell after years of research, to be pure urban legend.

Like everyone else, though, we didn't realize that at first. But since what we saw on the Internet was the opposite of the actual studies we were looking at, we set out to trace the numbers quoted in books, magazine articles, blogs, and news stories, expecting that we would find at least some good sources worth discussing. For example, an online search of "divorce rate second marriages" turned up dozens of seemingly solid statements, like the opening of this 2012 online article from *Psychology Today:*

Past statistics have shown that in the U.S. 50 percent of first marriages, 67 percent of second, and 73 percent of third marriages end in divorce. What are the reasons for this progressive increase in divorce rates?[85]

What we noticed very quickly was that most of the articles and books we looked at either cited no sources or cited articles (such as the *Psychology Today* piece above) that themselves cited no sources. We did find a few writers who had in good faith cited and re-cited more solid-seeming data sources, only to discover, when we dug further, that those sources either didn't exist or didn't say any such thing. We saw three such examples over and over.

Dozens of reporters and other writers had referenced Jennifer Baker of the School of Professional Psychology at Forest Institute in Springfield, Missouri, as being the source of those high divorce numbers. We contacted Dr. Baker to ask about her findings, and she quickly e-mailed us: "Unfortunately, these statistics are not mine, and even though I have asked the website to remove my name as a source, I've been unable to get them to do so."[86]

Other writers referenced a particular 2006 Census Bureau table as the source for a 60 percent and 73 percent divorce rate for second marriages and third marriages, respectively. (Yay! An actual citation!) But when we dug into the Census Bureau reports to find the table in question, we discovered it didn't contain those numbers. Perplexed, we called the relevant department at the census (they knew us well by now) and asked for their help. After hours of experimenting with the data to see whether there was some obscure way to come up with those percentages from that table, the census folks confirmed the percentages simply didn't exist.[87] One of the long-tenured census staff members (who adhered to the census policy of not being quoted by name) said emphatically, "Those aren't our numbers. We did look, but they're just not there. The Census Bureau is quoted as being the source for a million things incorrectly." This source said that there is always the possibility that someone may have somehow estimated those numbers on their own and used census data in some way, but the numbers themselves are not from the Census Bureau. They simply may have spread because they looked official.

Finally, we saw several times the citation "US Bureau of Statistics, 1995" as showing what percent of marriages each year are remarriages, but there is no such agency in the United States (although there is in Australia). Even among the US government departments that do keep vital statistics, we have found no such numbers.

It is possible that the 60 percent / 73 percent redivorce rate myth could have been fueled by misunderstandings about studies that were analyzing issues *other* than divorce rates and looking at high-risk groups on purpose.[88] It is also very possible that people have looked at the alarming *projections* some concerned researchers made back in the high-divorce years of the 1980s and believed that those studies were reporting *actual* divorce rates for second and third marriages.[89] And finally, it is also quite possible that despite our efforts there are other studies we are simply missing. But as of this writing, Tally and I have not been able to locate a single actual data set or study that has researched the matter and concluded that the remarriage divorce rate is in the 60 percent / 73 percent ballpark.

## Circling Closer to the Truth

One of the premier marriage and divorce researchers, Andrew Cherlin of Johns Hopkins University, captured the difficulty in understanding remarriage divorce trends in a 2010 *Journal of*

*Family and Marriage* article when he commented, "Few demographic analyses of trends in remarriage were published in the 2000s, so it is not known whether it became more or less common among the divorced population."[90]

The truth is that not only are recent data sets sparse, but remarriage research in general is meager. A few studies, however, give us solid-enough data to debunk the doom-and-gloom bad-news myths. Yes, remarriages appear to have a somewhat higher divorce rate (especially in the first five years), and yes, it makes a lot of sense for those who have already experienced a divorce to be particularly careful about avoiding another one. But the evidence also shows that remarriages (especially second marriages) can be expected to last a lifetime.

Let's take a quick look at three of these studies.

## Study 1: Census Bureau, 2009—Just as 71 Percent of Women Are Still Married to Their First Spouse, 65 Percent Are Still Married to Their Second Spouse[91]

One of the most telling statistics for remarriages is the percent of them that are still intact. According to the 2009 US Census Bureau SIPP survey that we looked at earlier, 71 percent of women (and 72 percent of people overall) are still married to their first spouse.[92] And the percent for second marriages isn't dramatically different: 65 percent of women in their second marriages are still married to that spouse. Among the 35 percent who aren't, those marriages are even more likely than first marriages to end in the death of a spouse because these marriages often started at older ages.[93]

When we look at this data, there is no way to know the numbers for the rate of divorce rather than death, but it will certainly be significantly lower than 35 percent. And it is good news that at *most* the divorce rate for second marriages is only six percentage points higher than the divorce rate for first marriages. (This is similar to the finding of a well-regarded, older study by Professor Emeritus Bumpass.)[94]

Although this is pure speculation, because second marriages are so much more likely than first marriages to end in death, it is analytically even possible that the actual long-term divorce rate among remarriages could be *lower* than for first marriages. Especially, as referenced below, once you get past the first few years of the second marriage. (See also endnote 94 about Larry Bumpass's study.)

Even among third marriages, the marriages-not-intact numbers are not the majority, as 59 percent of women on their third marriages are still married to that spouse (meaning 41 percent aren't, due to widowhood or divorce). For the full breakdown, see the table below.

### Intact Marriages

|  | Women | Men |
| --- | --- | --- |
| First marriage intact | 71% | 81% |
| Second marriage intact | 65% | 78% |
| Third marriage intact | 59% | 75% |

Source: US Census Bureau, 2009 SIPP, calculated from table 6.

## Study 2: Bureau of Labor Statistics, 2013—Even Among the High-Risk Baby Boomers, the Second-Marriage Divorce Rate Is 36 Percent[95]

The Bureau of Labor Statistics (BLS) studied the second-marriage divorce rates of a specific group of high-risk people: those born between 1957 and 1964—the end of the baby boom generation. What the researchers discovered resembles the SIPP numbers, that 62 percent of second marriages are still intact. But unlike the SIPP numbers, they studied which marriages ended due to divorce and which to widowhood, and discovered that an average of 36 percent of those second marriages had ended in divorce.

In this study, the divorce-rate difference between men and women is barely two percentage points (35.2 percent versus 37.4 percent), suggesting again that the big difference between men and women in the SIPP data is mainly due to widowhood of more women. This is encouraging, given that this group is one of the highest-risk cohorts, and thus other age groups are likely to have lower divorce-rate numbers for second marriages.

In other words, the reality is essentially the opposite of the 60 percent myth.

## Study 3: CDC Report, 2002—in Second Marriages, the Divorce Rate by the Tenth Anniversary Is Only Six Percentage Points Higher Than That of First Marriages[96]

In chapter 2, we mentioned the CDC's highly studied National Survey of Family Growth, which heavily surveyed those who married young. Although the raw divorce rates from this group aren't nationally representative for age, as with the SIPP, it is one of the few studies that breaks out divorce rates of first and second marriages, and the *difference* between those groups within the study is still valuable, even if the actual divorce-rate numbers are not. Among women who divorced within ten years of getting married (the longest period available), the second-marriage divorce rate was only six percentage points higher than that of first marriages.[97]

This study also shows that just as with first marriages, the greatest divorce risk for remarriages comes in the first five years. Another well-respected demographer named Joshua Goldstein points out that, specifically, "divorce rates peak during the fourth year for both first marriages and remarriages."[98] Those who have made it to their second marriage's fifth anniversary have a much greater chance of their marriage lasting a lifetime.

So beyond the baby boomer numbers found by the Bureau of Labor Statistics, and other than the CDC numbers of those married young, what might the actual divorce rate be for a more representative cross section of remarriages? A "Family Profile" published by the National Center for Family and Marriage Research at Bowling Green State University, under codirectors Wendy Manning and Susan Brown, found that when lumping all remarriages together (including second, third, fourth marriages, and more), the divorce rate for first marriages is 35 percent lower than for all remarriages.[99] In chapter 2, we estimated that roughly one in four first marriages have ended in divorce.

A 35 percent increase would imply that on average about one in three of all remarriages would end in divorce.

> This implies that on average about one in three remarriages would end in divorce.

## Determined to Be Different

About a year after I first started this research, I learned something about one of my close friends that stunned me. She and her husband (I'll call him Brady) had been friends with Jeff and me for years. They had been married for more than thirty years, their kids were grown, and we often turned to them for advice and prayer on many issues of life.

One night over dinner, we were talking about this research and the myth of the remarriage divorce rate, and I saw my friend and her husband exchange a look that I couldn't read.

"What?" I asked.

"Well..." She smiled ruefully. "Did you know that I was married before?"

I must have looked stunned. "I had no idea."

"I was married for all of eighteen months. We were so young. We made every mistake you can make. I wasn't going to church. It just fell apart. I really thought I would be secondhand goods forever. And then a few years later, I met Brady."

To my consternation, suddenly her eyes filled with tears.

"Every day I thank God for Brady. I cannot imagine life without him. The pain of having done it wrong, and seeing how good it can be when you do it right, when you do what God asks… It is the greatest possible reason for us to know that in this marriage we will be together forever."

A marriage and family pastor I was briefing on this shared something similar. He said,

A first marriage is optimal, is God's intent for marriage. But God is also so kind to those who have been young and stupid and done everything wrong. By God's grace I see so often that He gives those on their second chance a rich and wonderful marriage.

I meet people all the time who have been married twenty or thirty years and have a great marriage. And when I get to know them, I learn that "Well you know this was my second marriage. I was married at twenty-two and divorced by twenty-five."

I'm constantly surprised in looking at second marriages, even with the challenges of a blended family, at how happy they are. They say, "I was so immature before. But I learned my lesson, and this time is different. This time, I knew what to look for. What I need to change."

Although divorce leaves many scars and second marriages come with unique challenges, the "I've learned my lesson, and this time is different" reaction is one reason that I see hope in the most recent BLS study and the Census Bureau's second-marriage data above. Although the divorce rate may be higher for re-marriages, especially in the first few years, I think *many* remarried couples are actually less likely to divorce the second time around. They feel like they have, in my friend's words, "done it wrong" once, and they are determined not to do that again. They are committed for life.

## Giving Hope

Knowing the good news may, in the end, make it easier for them to keep that commitment. After having been a single mom for years, another friend of mine just got remarried. After reading a draft of this chapter, she e-mailed me this:

> This is so personal for me coming into a remarriage that I truly hope will be a blessed and happy marriage. I find that I have this subconscious fear, especially when there is conflict and things aren't going well. Fear that I am responsible. Fear that I will make a mistake. Fear that I need a backup plan, that I must protect my kids if something goes wrong. Maybe all that fades after the first five years and you don't worry about all the "what ifs" each time. But that is where communication, trust, and prayer play such a large role in remarriage. You come into it already damaged once.
>
> I realize I have to work constantly to make sure I stay

open to my husband and do not slide into protective
mode when I am worried, hurt, upset, or tired. To me,
the hopeful message of the book is something that will
help so much. This hope will be one of the things I look
toward when I am sliding toward protecting myself or my
kids; it will help me to stop that trend and instead lean
into my marriage and husband in the way we deserve.

Remember the remarried couple I quoted at the beginning of
the chapter? They said they made it due to the vision that they
had "of what it could be like if we chose to press on." And, they
said, "That gave us hope, although sometimes it was literally the
last thread we were holding on to."

A thread is better than nothing, but it seems so fragile. How
much more of that all-important hope might we give the two in
ten couples who are remarried if they knew that they had a much
greater chance of making it than they thought?

## Summary

- Most people, including leaders, erroneously believe
  that 60 percent of second marriages and 73 percent
  of third marriages fail.
- We have tried for years to trace the sources for those
  numbers and have found that, as far as we can tell
  right now, they don't exist. They appear to be pure

urban legend, which is perpetuated in part because there simply aren't very many studies on remarriages and those that do exist aren't well known.

- According to 2009 Census Bureau data, just as 71 percent of women are still married to their first spouse, 65 percent of women are still married to their second spouse.

- Among the 35 percent who aren't still married to their second spouse, a much larger percentage of that is probably due to death than in first marriages, simply because these couples tend to be older. In fact, it is analytically possible that especially after the first few high-risk years, the remarriage divorce rate could be *lower* than for first marriages.

- According to the data we do have, and what we can infer from various studies, roughly one-third of second marriages appear to end in divorce.

## Good News #4

The large majority of remarriages last. Among women in second marriages, 65 percent are still married to their spouse, and of those who aren't, many were widowed rather than divorced.

# 6

# It's the Little Things

## How Most Marriage Problems Can Be Fixed by Small Changes

After the release of my book *For Women Only*, people began sharing the most rewarding stories about couples whose marriages had been saved, changed, or restored through the knowledge they gained from that research. In the same way that I had been astonished by what I was learning about men (especially Jeff) while I was writing it, my female readers seemed to suddenly see something they simply didn't know before. As I began speaking at women's conferences, countless women were relaying stories of how they would read the book in bed next to their husband, come across a finding about men that shocked them, turn to their man, and say, "Is this true?" Upon hearing (most of the time) yes, that was true, they would begin a deep conversation and discover things about their man that they hadn't learned in twenty-five years of marriage, usually things their husband hadn't known how to articulate. And upon the release of the corresponding book about women, *For Men Only,* the aha moments went both ways. Using these discoveries, men and women started to change what they did and said to align with what they now understood about their spouse.

What I was continuously struck by, though—in their lives and in mine—was how *simple* the changes often were. It was as if, with a little bit of extra knowledge about their spouse, people could scoot themselves into a whole new realm of marriage. Some folks already had a good marriage, while others had been unhappy for years; but either way just a few eye-opening pieces of information somehow allowed these men and women to help themselves instead of feeling helpless.

And early on, I heard a story that clued me in to the fact that there was an even bigger implication behind this trend, an implication that has a vital part to play in countering the current sense of futility about marriage.

After twelve years of marriage, a couple we'll call Nelly and Brad had separated. Although neither started out believing in divorce, he had given up on the idea of ever being able to please her, and as he grew more and more distant, she became more and more critical and was convinced he had a personality disorder that made him narcissistic.

Finally Brad gave up. He rented an apartment closer to his trucking company's headquarters about two hours away. By this point, things were so bad between them that his only regret was being so far away from their twin four-year-old daughters. He told me later, "That was what really killed me—the idea of not being able to see my girls all the time."

About two months later, on the road in his rig, he caught a few minutes of a radio interview where I discussed *For Women Only* and what I learned about how men think. He was astonished, not because of what I shared about men's fears and needs, but because it sounded as though women didn't already know what they were.

The next day, on the last leg home, he happened to walk into a truck stop and see the companion book, *For Men Only*, on a spinner rack. After reading a few chapters over lunch, he headed out—not to his apartment, but to the house he had shared with his wife. He walked in, opened up the book, pointed to several passages, and said, "Is this true of *you*?"

Suddenly, both of them started talking. He suddenly understood so many things that weren't just his wife's issues but were common to *most* women. He saw how much certain actions of his had hurt her...and how much she *hadn't* realized she was hurting him!

And on her part, Nelly began to see that what she took as his ego was actually a deep self-doubt and longing to be appreciated. They spent most of the night discussing things they had never known before, and the next day, he drove down to his apartment, packed his things, and came home.

I was so touched when he shared his story with me. But as I heard another like it...and another...I began to realize, *If just a little bit of new knowledge can save a marriage, there are a whole lot of unnecessary divorces going on.*

If just a little bit of new knowledge can save a marriage, there are a whole lot of unnecessary divorces going on.

### It's Usually Not the Big-Ticket Problems

As noted in chapter 3, most marriages, thankfully, are happy. More than a third, in fact, are very happy. But as I've conducted my interviews and surveys with those men and women who are "mostly happy" or in "so-so or struggling" marriages, I frequently hear something important under the surface, a feeling that I can only describe as a combination of confusion and helplessness. That feeling of *He's upset with me and I don't know why* or *I can't seem to really make her happy, no matter how hard I try.*

That sense of confusion and helplessness is just one step removed from a sense of futility. The feeling that having a good marriage or fixing a troubled one requires a PhD in clinical psychology with a minor in mind reading. And it is that helpless feeling that is so often quickly blown away by simply having a little information the couple didn't have before.

The good-news truth that Jeff and I have seen over the years, that Brad and Nelly's story hints at and that countless counselors have confirmed, is that most marriage breakdowns are not caused by what you might call the deep, systemic big-ticket problems—

for example, by one spouse being an alcoholic or having been sexually abused as a child. Those problems do happen and it is tragic when they do, but they aren't the majority of cases. Instead, what usually happens is that a husband and wife who deeply care about each other are tripped up by some relatively simple things, often resulting from a lack of knowledge about what the other person needs or what hurts them. They simply don't know some elementary needs and fears shared by not only their spouse but most other men or women, or they don't know a few simple day-to-day actions that would make a big difference to the happiness of the marriage.

Let's look at two intertwined good-news truths I've seen in the research.

## Truth 1: More Than 99 Percent of Spouses Deeply Care About Each Other

In our research for *The Surprising Secrets of Highly Happy Marriages,* Jeff and I identified several simple things that the happiest spouses do that they often don't even realize are making them so happy.[100] And one of the most important is that they try to believe the best of their spouse's intentions even when they have been hurt.

We found in our research that the vast majority of spouses—more than 99 percent overall, and only a few points less even in troubled marriages—care deeply about their mate (see graph, next page).[101] The problem is their mate doesn't always believe it.

Out of the 1,261 people who have answered that completely

anonymous survey question, only *nine people* said they didn't really care about their spouse anymore. Not 9 percent—nine people! Even in the most troubled marriages, 97 percent of the survey takers said they cared about their spouse. And yet of those spouses, only 59 percent believed it. That gap is a major reason for all the unnecessary unhappiness and angst in marriage. A hurting spouse thinks *He* [or *She*] *doesn't care about me*—but that just isn't true!

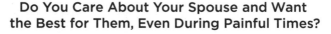

**Do You Care About Your Spouse and Want the Best for Them, Even During Painful Times?**

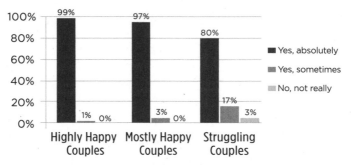

Indeed, our *For Women Only* and *For Men Only* surveys revealed how much people really do care about their mates. When we gave the men and women an open-ended space and essentially asked, "What's the one most important thing you wish your spouse knew?" we were surprised and touched to see that the top answer by far for the men were comments that relayed "how much I love her," and the top answer for women were comments that conveyed that "he is my hero."

We have seen conclusively that most of us care about our spouses and want the best for them. We want our mates to be happy. And in most cases, we not only *feel* that caring feeling toward our spouses, but we are trying hard to *show* that we care. We are trying to do the right things.

The problem is that most of us are, without realizing it, also carrying around some incorrect assumptions about what our spouses need, usually because we don't inherently know a few deeply buried but vital needs and insecurities of the opposite sex. So when we try to do the right things, all too often we are trying hard in the wrong areas and not making the other person feel cared for in the way we think we are. All too often our spouses aren't feeling the way we think they should feel after all our hard work. And unfortunately, sometimes we are even *hurting* the other person without ever realizing it.

All of this is why a little new knowledge can make such a big difference. Once someone learns a key fact about what their spouse needs (or what hurts them), they can try hard in the *right* areas. They can avoid hurting the person who matters most to them.

## Truth 2: In 82 Percent of Struggling Couples, One Partner Is Simply Unaware the Other Is Not Happy

You may remember from the Linda Waite study mentioned in chapter 3 that when the most deeply hurting couples stuck with their marriages, eight in ten of them were happily married five years later. Those kinds of turnarounds demonstrate just how unlikely it is that most of those problems were deep-rooted, highly complex issues.[102]

Instead, one of the reasons that sticking with it is probably so effective is something that I found in our nationally representative survey.[103] In 82 percent of the so-so or struggling marriages, one of the partners didn't seem to realize their spouse was actually not happy. Couples in which both people answered that they weren't happy comprised only *four percentage points* out of the 22 percent of couples who were listed as struggling. In all the rest, one partner said he or she was happy. This is a high degree of simply not being clued in to a partner's unhappiness.

## Marriages Where One or Both Spouses Are Less Than Happy

| | |
|---|---|
| Both partners agree they are less than happy | 18% |
| One spouse thinks the marriage is happy | 82% |

Source: Data from *The Surprising Secrets of Highly Happy Marriages* study, Shaunti Feldhahn, 2013.

As odd as it sounds, I see this as hopeful. It would seem to be far easier to get one slightly oblivious and one hurting person to change than to get two people entrenched in anger and hurt to change. It is a lot easier to solve a lack of awareness than alcoholism. Remember, even the most hurting spouses usually care about and want the best for their mates. Sure, there are also some marriages ruined by inconsiderate jerks who simply don't care, but that is a tiny percentage of the total. In most cases, just because a spouse doesn't truly *see* something, it doesn't mean he or she doesn't care.

> It is a lot easier to solve a lack of awareness than alcoholism.

Not long ago, I was sharing this research with Emerson Eggerichs, who wrote the groundbreaking book *Love and Respect* and whose input has been extraordinarily helpful to my research over the years. When I referred to a high degree of "cluelessness" among one spouse in 82 percent of those struggling couples, he quickly stopped me. "That word gives completely the wrong impression," he said. "It implies someone who is disengaged, uncaring, and out of touch. I'm guessing that the person who doesn't 'see' the problem is more likely to be the husband, but he's not uncaring. He cares about his wife deeply. He would die for her. The problem is he doesn't necessarily know how to live for her. For example, he is working seventy-hour weeks to provide and say 'I love you' and doesn't know that she's getting more and more unhappy because she wants more time with *him*. So he is trying hard but is missing the mark, and doesn't know how to fix it. This is why your work and mine makes such a big difference. It is turning on the light bulb, so he *does* know how to fix it."

If indeed most problems require intervention but not rocket science, and if one can "wake up" or educate one or both spouses and restore commitment, it makes sense that a few changes should be able to make a big difference. It makes sense that within five years a couple could have gone from very unhappy to very happy.

## A Case Study Close to Home

What might a "few changes that make a big difference" look like? I'll give you an example that hits very close to home—the classic love-respect disconnect that Jeff and I surveyed men and women about and that Emerson details in *Love and Respect*. The classic disconnect that I, it turns out, had in full measure.

Like most wives, I love my husband very much, and through the years frequently said "I love you" to Jeff and did loving things; it just poured out of me naturally. But I had no idea that while he thought that was nice, it didn't have nearly the impact for him that respect did—for example, knowing that I appreciated him or chose to trust him.

In fact, like three out of four men on my eventual survey for *For Women Only,* Jeff needed respect so much he would give up love to get it. But I didn't realize that, or how much he needed to see that I trusted him as a good father, or how great it felt to hear me say appreciative things like "Thank you for working so hard to support the family." I rarely showed him that sort of overt appreciation. Even though I certainly felt it inside, I didn't think to *say* it. In other words, I was, without realizing it, working hard in the wrong areas and simply wasn't making Jeff feel truly cared for like I thought I was. I was, in fact, clueless. (I can say that about myself!)

And worse, I often made him feel very *un*cared for. Not realizing that a man's most painful feeling is insecurity, I would question his decisions all the time or tease him in front of others. I had no idea he would, as he says now, "rather chew broken glass" than endure some of my "harmless" jokes in front of those he cared about and wanted to respect him. To my shame, and like all too many other women, I thought he was oversensitive. I thought those things shouldn't bother him. And it wasn't until I first stumbled into this area of research that I realized I was thinking that way simply because they wouldn't bother *me*.

What I had to learn was that my husband was very, very different from me. And (I hate to confess this) I also had to recognize that not only did his emotional needs and insecurities exist, but they were just as legitimate as my own. Like many women, I simply didn't know that the vast majority of men were just like him.

And Jeff, like many other men, had things he simply didn't know about me, needs and insecurities he didn't realize were legitimate and common to most women. Once we began learning these things, everything in our marriage changed. We hadn't come close to divorce like Brad and Nelly, but we certainly had many unhappy days. We had many nights where one of us would sleep in the guest bedroom because we couldn't bear to sleep next to the person who should care about us the most but didn't seem to care about us at all. We had whole vacations spoiled by being carefully polite on the outside in front of others while seething with anger or hurt on the inside.

Like so many other marriages, ours was hurting due to

something as tragically stupid as a lack of the right information. And as with so many others, all that changed for us once we learned these few things we didn't know before. It didn't happen overnight, of course. On my side, for example, it took me years to unlearn the damaging habit of telling Jeff exactly how I wanted him to do things: how to drive, where to park, how to dress our kids, what he should have said in the business meeting—all the things that tell any man "You're an idiot" without his wife ever realizing it. It took me years to get into the habit of not just feeling but saying thank you (important to 98 percent of men), to recognize the self-doubt he had inside (like 75 percent of men), or to see that physical intimacy was (as for 97 percent of men) primarily an emotional need for him.

And Jeff had his own unlearning and relearning to do, such as recognizing that to me (as with 70 percent of all other married women), his seventy-hour workweeks to support the family weren't nearly as important as ensuring the two of us were close. Or pulling himself out of a funk when he was in a bad mood (important to 97 percent of women), or reassuring me that "We're okay" if we were in conflict (like 95 percent of women).[104]

But notice, none of those things were big-ticket, systemic issues. None required a PhD to solve. As HomeWord founder Jim Burns once told us, the types of things that we found in our research that people didn't always know were "truths that were hidden in plain sight."

We did seek counsel at times, and we did need help in understanding how to *apply* what we were learning, but ultimately, with some new knowledge and appreciation about what the other person most needed and was most hurt by, we could help ourselves. We didn't have that helpless feeling anymore. Marriage didn't have to be so hard.

## The Hope of the Simple Solution

We have since seen that pattern repeated literally thousands of times in our research, and it is just as important of a good-news truth as a lower divorce rate or a higher rate of happiness. The idea that it will take years of work, pain, complicated effort, and three-times-a-week counseling to fix something is enough to discourage far too many couples before they start. Of course, we know that in some cases, many years of hard, slogging efforts are indeed required. But in most cases, those fears are exaggerated; in most cases, the sun can shine through the storm clouds much more quickly. We know that...but many couples don't.

> Most couples don't mind the idea of working hard at marriage. What discourages them is the idea that marriage *itself* is inherently hard and complicated, or that working hard won't pay off.

In my experience—and probably in yours—most couples don't mind the idea of working hard at marriage. What discourages them is the idea that marriage *itself* is inherently hard and complicated, or that working hard won't pay off. Because that implies that a truly delightful marriage simply isn't realistic for the average couple.

One young couple I know has been together for ten years, has two children, and has no plans to get married. She would like to, but he is skeptical. "What does the piece of paper matter?" he says. "We have children. We love each other. That should be enough."

When I asked him why he thought the piece of paper—the legal marriage—didn't matter, he looked at me as politely as he could while also looking at me like I was crazy. "Most marriages break up, and most married couples argue all the time. Why would I want some of that? It's better as we are. Keep it simple. Keep it simple."

While I privately suspect that disdain for the "piece of paper" is a subconscious way to hide his understandable fear of a full commitment that he worries he'll be inadequate to uphold, his comments are a pretty good indication of just how much *all* the good-news truths we've talked about are needed in today's culture.

So with that in mind, let's take a deep breath and transition from the five good-news facts to what a difference it would make in our culture if everyone knew the truth of them.

## Summary

- Often, the actions needed to make a great marriage, or to turn around a struggling one, are simple.

- Most marriage problems are not caused by the big-ticket issues like addiction but from a buildup of misunderstandings, conflict, and hurt feelings. Often, both spouses just didn't know some elementary needs and fears shared by not only their mate but by most of their spouse's gender, so they hurt their mate without intending to.

- More than 99 percent of married people care deeply about their spouse.

- In 82 percent of struggling couples, one partner is simply unaware that their spouse is less than happy, which is a lot easier to address than both people being entrenched in hurt.

- Couples typically don't mind working hard at marriage. What discourages them is the thought that marriage itself is inherently hard or complicated, or that working hard won't make a difference. This is why it is so encouraging when they see that a few simple changes can make a big difference.

## Good News #5

In most cases, having a good marriage or improving a struggling one doesn't have to be ultra-complicated or solve deep, systemic issues; small changes can and do often make a big difference.

# 7

# The Power of Hope

## What a Difference the Good News Makes

When I got my first car, I wanted something cute and unique. Being twenty-three years old and about to leave for graduate school, I didn't have a lot of money, but I wanted as appealing and unique as I could get for the price. I found a perky little Isuzu with a stylish shape, and—even better—it was white. That was cool, I thought, since most people don't have white cars. But as soon as I drove it off the lot, guess what happened. I started seeing white cars everywhere! At first I was bummed that suddenly there were so many out there. Then I realized that there wasn't actually a craze for white cars; I was just noticing them more. Now that I was predisposed to see them, they took on more weight in my mind.

That same psychological principle applies to how we think about marriage and divorce. Just as with my white car, when we believe that so many marriages end in divorce, we notice the divorces more. *Yep, there's another one.*

We see them everywhere and subconsciously begin to think of them as the rule rather than the exception. So instead of mourning the ones that do happen as tragic exceptions, we give a fatalistic shrug. That leads to a negative spiral; as we give the marital breakdowns more weight, we don't notice or give a lot of credence to the truly happy marriages that are (as you now know) the vast majority. We develop a sense of discouragement about an institution and a relationship that God designed to be one of the greatest blessings of our lives.

But we can change that pattern. Thankfully, the same psychological principle applies to how we think about the good news as well. Once you are geared to notice it, you'll see it everywhere.

## Noticing the Good Around Every Corner

What a difference it will make for people to begin to notice the positive news that they just didn't see before, the encouraging data that really is there around every corner. For example, imagine the vast difference for the young person who hears the positive data one week, goes to church the next, looks around, and thinks, *Most of the people in here have happy marriages—how cool. There really is something great that happens when you do marriage God's way.*

Imagine the vast difference for the struggling husband or wife who passes a happy couple on the street holding hands and thinks, *If we work at it, we can get back to that,* instead of thinking, *They're the exception.*

Imagine the difference for someone reading a news story provocatively titled "Divorce After 50 Grows More Common" who is clued in enough to notice that buried in all the doom and gloominess designed to sell papers is the statement that it may be more common than before—but is still only 15 percent of that population![105]

> Imagine the vast difference for the young person who hears the positive data one week, goes to church the next, looks around, and thinks, *Most of the people in here have happy marriages—how cool.*

Imagine those patterns repeated in every community, in every church or synagogue, in every corner around the country. Do you think that will make a difference in how people feel about marriage?

Let me emphasize again: I am not in any way denying that there is still plenty of sobering information out there. None of what I've shown you is evidence that we've been living in some sort of marriage utopia all along. The divorce rate is still too high. Too many marriages still do struggle. Some people give up too easily. Others are impacted by someone else's poor choices.

But for too long we've been giving that bad news more weight than it actually has in reality—and giving the good news too little. Jud Wilhite, the pastor of Las Vegas megachurch Central

Christian, put it this way when I shared this data with him: "People have been discouraged about marriage for so long. And yes, there are still problems; you make that clear. But people already *know* the problems! What they don't know is some of the good stuff. That simple sense of hope is like a drink of water to some very thirsty people."

## Thirsty People Looking for Water

If God really has put a longing for an abundant, joyful, happy marriage in the human heart, then it is no wonder that people are thirsty for good news, for that sense of hope instead of futility. But I also think it is part of a bigger story. In this divided, stressful day and age, I think people are thirsty for good news of *all* kinds.

I see that exemplified in the history of the company that makes my favorite clothes: those casual, stonewashed T-shirts with the "Life is good" slogan. In 1994, the same year I was graduating from grad school in Boston and marrying my husband, the founders of that company were experiencing their own life-changing moment across town. Brothers Bert and John Jacobs were designing T-shirts and selling them door to door to college students out of the back of a minivan, but they weren't making much progress and were thinking of giving it up.

On one road trip, they got into a discussion about how the news on TV always seems to be negative, focusing on what is wrong—and yet, they thought, people were thirsty for good news. So, they drew a little stick figure they named Jake, a guy who was smiling and looked like he enjoyed life, a guy who could figure things out. Underneath Jake, they put the slogan "Life is good." They printed up forty-eight T-shirts, took them to the streets of Boston...and sold out in forty-five minutes. They realized how much people need signals of hope and good news, and that is the need on which they have since built a $100 million company. As Bert said, "That was the day that changed everything."[106]

I've seen that need too. As I share this information, people latch on to it—not with the look of someone coolly thinking *Oh, how very interesting,* but in some cases with the look of a drowning person who has been tossed a life preserver.

People are truly longing for good news. Not the "let's just put a good face on things" kind, but the truly good news we subconsciously know must be out there somewhere, if God really has promised that He wants good things for us.

## "The Implications Are Enormous"

I mentioned earlier that the first time I publicly shared this data was at a conference for pastors and leaders who worked with marriages and families. One marriage ministry leader came up to me afterward and said, "If this is true, the implications are enormous."

I have heard that many times since then, and they are right—

the implications are enormous! With this news, we have a way to reassure a struggling couple that they can get their happy marriage back. We can confidently say "Going to church does matter." Talking to an unmarried couple who says "Why bother getting married?" we can confidently say "Because once you commit for life, you're much likelier to be happy and enjoy your relationship!" But perhaps the most significant, personal implication is knowing with certainty that we can still believe in marriage.

With that knowledge, we can begin to do things differently. In fact, we *will* begin to do things differently. When I shared this information with the event coordinator at a recent women's conference, she surprised me when she instantly said, "This is so practical." When I asked what she meant, she explained that her background was in counseling, then said, "This isn't just esoteric knowledge; it is day-to-day practical. Because most of us just act the way we see things. You do what you know. So when you see something differently, that becomes the new normal and you act differently as a result."

> "You can believe in marriage" can be the new normal. Yes, the implications of that are enormous for what we do as individuals—and as leaders.

"You can believe in marriage" can be the new normal. Yes, the implications of that are enormous for what we do as individuals—and as leaders.

## The Difference It Makes for Leaders

Those who work in the marriage arena, whether directly with couples or in a bigger-picture way such as policy development, are thought leaders, meaning their thoughts and perceptions about marriage and divorce directly influence what others will think. One therapist gave a great example of how a small change in the perception of a leader can mean a dramatic ripple-effect shift for everyone else:

> In the first few sessions of marital therapy, I have one goal: de-escalating what is going on. As part of that, I am holding the hope for them. As therapists, that is our role. These couples usually don't have that hope when they come in, and they are looking to us to help them find it again. So if we feel more hope, they will too.

What a leader chooses to do and say will often change in a very concrete way once they know some of these facts that they just didn't know before. As one marriage counselor put it,

> For the last fifteen years, I've been held hostage by numbers I couldn't argue with. I've done my best, but I was basically putting a good spin on things. But knowing that the great news is out there, I can actually show a couple the numbers that so many marriages are happy, or that it really is possible to become happy if you stick to it.

That's liberating. It's like the difference between a doctor saying "You've got cancer, but with this type of cancer, most people make it" and having to say "You've got cancer and we'll fight it, but the odds aren't great."

The good news is also personally encouraging for pastors and others who work with a body of people and are already working hard to support marriages. One told me, "You know what this does? In a weird way, it actually allows me to relax a bit. I really have felt that what we were doing at our church *was* working. It didn't match the numbers I'd *heard,* but it matched what I *saw* around me. I would suggest to pastors: if what you're doing is working, don't second-guess yourself. For example, Weekend to Remember conferences or Love and Respect conferences have enormous benefit. You don't need to redesign what is clearly working." He thought for a moment and then continued, "And do a survey. I think that's my next step. To know the real-deal needs we should add or adjust, rather than guessing."

Another told me knowing this information was a relief for a completely different reason:

I was the marriage and family pastor for about ten years and just took over as senior pastor a year ago. But in all that time, we've primarily been reacting to problems. Partly because we thought that *was* what was most needed, but also partly because I'm not sure we believed it was possible to make such a wholesale difference. So it is *huge* to find out that we don't need to make a wholesale difference! I don't need to change 50 or 60 or 70 percent of the congregation—I only need in-depth help for 5 percent, maybe 10 percent, and encouragement and community support for everyone else. That is doable.

## "For Relationships, It Always Comes Down to Hope"

Not long ago at an event in New England, I sat down with Paul Friesen, author, with his wife, Virginia, of *The Marriage App* and a leader, therapist, and pastor who had encouraged me in this research years ago. I wanted to brief him and Virginia on the results of this long investigative study, especially since they were there near the very beginning and had heard some very early results. I asked them for their perspective as authors, speakers, and therapists in the marriage arena. A few days later he sent me a long e-mail. I am going to conclude with his message in its entirety because it so perfectly captures the transforming power of hope:

For relationships, it always comes down to hope. Hebrews 11:1 says, "Now faith is confidence in what we hope for and assurance about what we do not see." Faith is tied to what is hoped for. This makes a lot of practical sense. If there is no hope, there will be little faith; if there is little faith, there will be little healing.

Our daughter is an athletic trainer. And after a serious injury, an athlete will always say something like, "Is there any hope I will play again?" The answer to that question will greatly affect the effort of the athlete in the healing process and will actually affect the trainer's suggested regimen for the athlete.

I believe the same is true in ministry. For most couples in serious turmoil, the first two questions they ask us are, "Have you ever seen a couple as bad as we are?" And "Is there any hope?" If therapists really do not have hope that a marriage can be renewed, I honestly feel our expectations are low and we do not "give it our best shot" nor is the couple motivated to do the work necessary. In essence, we decide to call hospice rather than the surgeon. We end up just coming alongside the couple as they divorce.

But if we truly believe in God's power to change and transform, we have not only hope that it *can* change but faith that it *will* change!

If couples have more hope, they will come for counsel earlier. After all, if we believe a disease can be cured if caught early, we are much more likely to check ourselves in than if we feel *there is no hope, so why go through the misery of the treatment?*

One couple came to us after three therapists told them there was no hope. We told them there is *always* hope if both wish to save the marriage. That was sixteen years ago, and they are still married, and now leading marriage classes.

Most couples will stay married (or not) based on marital satisfaction not marital statistics. *However,* I do believe statistics will have an effect on how they approach marriage to begin with, as well as how they continue to fight for their marriage. And that is far more likely to give them the marriage that they are hoping for. There are very few areas of life that impact us more, day to day, than our relationships. Telling people that there *are* those things that are excellent and beautiful and worthy of praise—pointing them out, so they know they are there—gives them exactly what they need to hold on to as they walk this life together.

At the end of the day, we need to truly grasp the goodness that God wants to give us as we hope in Him. We need to truly grasp the power of the Gospel to heal and give us life (and marriages!) to the full.

I believe that truly is God's intent for us and for our marriages. Now that we know that the news isn't all bad…that there is much that is excellent, and beautiful, and worthy of praise…let us see what a difference it makes when *that* becomes our new normal.

## Summarizing *The Good News About Marriage*

Following are the most important good-news findings, estimates, and conclusions in this book. My goal is to provide something helpful and quick for the busy marriage therapist, pastor, priest, counselor, or other reader who wants a crib sheet on what we found. Contrary to popular opinion, the good news is that...

**The actual divorce rate has never gotten close to 50 percent.** There is no way to nail down one final divorce rate. However, according to the Census Bureau,[i] 72 percent of people today are still married to their first spouse. And among the 28 percent who aren't, a portion of those marriages ended in widowhood, not divorce. Thus, the current divorce rate is probably closer to 20 to 25 percent for first marriages and 31 percent for all marriages (first and subsequent marriages). According to the same census report, 30.8 percent of ever-married women have been divorced. Many other studies have found similar numbers.[ii]

**Most marriages are happy.** Although most people think that only about a third of marriages are happy, in reality around 80 percent of marriages are happy. In multiple surveys, 91 to 97 percent of respondents say their marriages are happy.[iii] In my own survey that categorized couples based on the answers of *both* the husband and the wife (including, perhaps, a slightly higher number of distressed couples), 71 percent of couples were happy, with 34 percent being very happy.[iv] In another poll, 93 percent said they would marry their spouse all over again.[v] Encouragingly, if those who are most *un*happy stick with it, they rate their marriages as the most happy within five years.[vi]

**The rate of divorce in the church is not the same as the rate among those who don't attend worship services.** The common belief to the contrary is based on a misunderstanding of the well-known George Barna studies. In fact, every study that has been done has found that those who act on their faith by attending worship services, praying with their spouse, and so on are happier and closer in their marriage and/or have a significantly lower divorce rate. Several studies have found the rate of divorce among church attenders falls by roughly 25–50 percent.[vii] Special analysis of the Barna data shows that among those who attend church weekly, the divorce rate drops by 27 percent from those who do not.[viii]

**Most remarriages survive just fine.** Although popular myth puts the divorce rate for second marriages at over 60 percent and for third marriages at over 73 percent, these numbers appear to be purely urban legend. Census Bureau numbers show that 65 percent of women in second marriages are still married to their spouse, meaning only 35 percent of those marriages ended (and it is likely that a fairly significant percentage of those ended with the death of a spouse).[ix] In fact, the Bureau of Labor Statistics found that second marriages of a high-risk group of baby boomers had only a 36 percent divorce rate.[x] So we can estimate that roughly one-third of all remarriages have ended in divorce. The greatest spike in divorce in remarriages occurs within the first five years.[xi]

**Most marriage problems are not caused by big-ticket issues, and simple changes can make a big difference.** Most marriage problems are caused by day-to-day misunderstandings, unintended hurt, and trying hard in the wrong areas. Fully 99 percent of married people—and 97 percent even among struggling couples—care about their spouse and want the best for them. But in 82 percent of struggling couples, one partner is simply unaware of the other spouse's unhappiness.[xii] And since solving a lack of awareness is simpler than addressing major systemic issues, such as addiction, that is one reason why those who stick with tough marriages usually find themselves very happy five years later.

In summary, although there is plenty of very real concern surrounding the state of marriage in our culture today, many of the depressing "facts" that people think they know about marriage simply aren't true. After an eight-year study, we can firmly conclude that marriage is actually much stronger and happier than many of us have believed.

Getting this good news out there is vital for giving people hope, counteracting the dangerous feeling of futility about marriage that infects our culture, and demonstrating that we can still believe in marriage.

Visit www.goodnewsmarriage.com/leaders for a printable version of this and other tools. Enter the password "marriage" when prompted.

i. Rose M. Kreider and Renee Ellis, "Number, Timing, and Duration of Marriages and Divorces: 2009," *Current Population Reports* P70-125 (2011): 19, www.census.gov/prod/2011pubs/p70-125.pdf.

ii. For example, see University of Chicago, General Social Survey, 2012; University of Texas–Austin, the National Fatherhood Initiative Marriage Survey, 2005; the Barna Group, 2013.

iii. See, for example, University of Chicago, General Social Survey, multiple years; University of Texas–Austin, 2003–2004 survey for the National Fatherhood Initiative; Marist Poll 2010 for the Knights of Columbus.

iv. Shaunti Feldhahn, *The Surprising Secrets of Highly Happy Marriages* survey, conducted 2010–2012.

v. Norval D. Glenn, "With This Ring: A National Survey on Marriage in America," National Fatherhood Initiative, 2005, 34, http://blog.fatherhood.org/with-this-ring-survey. (The survey was conducted 2003–2004.)

vi. Linda J. Waite et al., *Does Divorce Make People Happy? Findings from a Study of Unhappy Marriages,* Institute for American Values, 2002, 5, https://docs.google.com/viewer?url=http://americanvalues.org/catalog/pdfs/does_divorce_make_people_happy.pdf.

vii. For example, see W. Bradford Wilcox, "Is Religion an Answer? Marriage, Fatherhood, and the Male Problematic," Research Brief No. 11 (New York: Institute for American Values, 2008), www.americanvalues.org/search/item.php?id=20; "When Baby Makes Three: How Parenthood Makes Life Meaningful and How Marriage Makes Parenthood Bearable," *The State of Our Unions 2011* (Charlottesville, VA: National Marriage Project at the University of Virginia, 2011), 31–32, figure 13, www.stateofourunions.org/2011/when-baby-makes-three.php; and Margaret L. Vaaler, Christopher G. Ellison, and Daniel A. Powers, "Religious Influences on the Risk of Marital Dissolution," *Journal of Marriage and Family* 71 (November 2009).

viii. Special analysis for Shaunti Feldhahn, 2008 OmniPoll, Barna Group, Ventura, CA, 2013.

ix. Kreider and Ellis, "Number, Timing, and Duration: 2009."

x. Alison Aughinbaugh, Omar Robles, and Hugette Sun, "Marriage and Divorce: Patterns by Gender, Race, and Educational Attainment," *Monthly Labor Review* (October 2013): table 3, section "Among Those Who Remarried After Divorce," www.bls.gov/opub/mlr/2013/article/marriage-and-divorce-patterns-by-gender-race-and-educational-attainment.htm. The BLS examined a specific cohort in the well-known longitudinal study National Longitudinal Survey of Youth 1979 (NLSY79).

xi. Joshua R. Goldstein, "The Leveling of Divorce in the United States," *Demography* 36, no. 3 (August 1999): 410–11, http://ccutrona.public.iastate.edu/psych592a/articles/Goldstein_1999.pdf.

xii. Shaunti Feldhahn, *The Surprising Secrets of Highly Happy Marriages* survey, conducted 2010–2012.

# "But What About...?"

## by Tally Whitehead

This Frequently Asked Questions section serves two purposes: First, to delve more deeply into some of the technical issues of the research, in a shorter Q&A style. Second, to answer the "But what about...?" questions that have frequently been asked as we have shared our findings across the country. There is so much that Shaunti and I could not fully cover in the previous chapters, so this section will hopefully give additional clarity and perhaps ease any lingering doubts over our assertions. To keep it simple, we have divided this FAQ chapter into sections about similar subjects.

Let the questioning begin!

### Rigor and Fairness

**Did you look at many studies for this book, and were you fair in trying to find studies that disagreed with your thesis that there is more good news than people think?**

Yes. Our overriding principle was that we wanted to get to the *truth,* whatever it was. Remember, we didn't start out looking for good news at all; we started out trying to find the technical information for Shaunti's columns and later, over the course of several years, for various articles on marriage and divorce. Shaunti did not wake up one day and think, *I'll bet the 50 percent divorce rate is a myth that I should debunk.* We looked at dozens (and eventually hundreds) of studies, data tables, and other pieces of research related to divorce, cohabitation, remarriage, and stepfamilies, and any faith-related studies that impact those life events. Through all the government statistics, academic journals, and church-oriented surveys, we became aware of the surprising facts that over and over again contradicted what we had once assumed.

However, remember that we are not claiming that there is no bad news out there. We are trying to bring balance to our culture's perception of marriage by stressing the good news that most people are not aware of or often overlook.

**Were you rigorous with examining all the studies equally, including "bad news" studies that challenge your premise or "good news" studies that might not actually have been done very well?**

Unequivocally. A big chunk of our time was spent analyzing the bad-news studies with higher divorce rates so we could understand where the 50 percent came from in the first place. Looking at all these studies closely was how we first realized that 50 percent was only a projection, not an ironclad measurement. Our goal was never to prove any experts wrong, because some of the earlier projections from the late 1970s honestly seemed plausible at the time, given how much divorce was increasing during those years. We just kept digging to find the whole truth and the current reality about marriage as well as we could. And as you saw in chapter 4, our research led us to rigorously research and debunk a few commonly stated pieces of *good* news as well (such as those who pray together have an ultra-low divorce rate).

Someone much smarter than we are once said it is Truth that sets us free. Marriages would not be helped by our delivering inaccurate good news! We simply searched for the truth, and that is what we have tried to present to the best of our ability.

## One Divorce for Every Two Marriages Each Year

**How can you state the divorce rate isn't 50 percent when there are half as many divorces as marriages annually?**

The people who get married in any given year are not the same people getting divorced in that same year (reality television stars aside), so half of those marriages are not ending. Look at it this way: If a pastor marries twenty couples in one year, but then has ten couples in his church divorce in that same year, is the church's divorce rate overall 50 percent? Of course not! (Unless there are only twenty couples in his church total.) Now, to keep the math simple, let's say that church has six hundred married couples. So out of six hundred married couples, ten have divorced in one year.

That means that church experienced a 1.6 percent rate of divorce for that year (10/600). Now, even if that pastor never marries another couple in that church ever again but ten more divorces occur every year, it would still take that church thirty years to reach a ratio of 50 percent divorced in their church.[107]

Nationally we have averaged about two marriages for every one divorce for decades.[108] In our example, that pastor's congregation may experience ten divorces every year, but the congregation would also probably continue to have twenty marriages added every year and thus would never get close to a 50 percent divorce rate. It works the same way in cities, counties, and the whole country.

**What about the divorces and marriages that take place in my city each year? Is there a way to calculate the divorce rate from those numbers?**

Let's use an example from a pastor who asked Shaunti a similar question. This pastor lives in a county that experienced 14,327 marriages and 7,760 divorces the prior year. He argued that this means his county has a 54 percent divorce rate. But remember that we can't look at the divorces that year as a percent of marriages that year (see above). Instead, you look at divorces that year as a percent of all the couples who *could* have gotten divorced that year, meaning all marriages in that county.

The correct way to calculate what percentage of couples experienced divorce for that year would be to take the number of divorces (7,760) and divide this number by the total number of marriages in that county. That county's website demographics section says 46.9 percent of the 807,621 households in this county consisted of married couples, which equals 378,774 married households. So those 7,760 divorces equaled about a 2 percent divorce rate for that year. (A note of caution about all these types of numbers: the National Vital Statistics System uses two different populations when calculating marriage and divorce rates, and so might this county.)[109] Other than divorces per year, the most likely way to find the prevalence of divorce in your area is if your local government publishes the "ever divorced" percentage from local surveys or vital statistics. And remember, the number of divorces will presumably include second, third, and fourth marriages, not just those of first marriages.

## But with Everyone Living Together…

**How relevant is your message about the good news in marriage when one of the main reasons divorce is dropping is because everyone is simply living together?**
Even though the cohabitation numbers are alarming to sociologists and pastors alike, first keep the big picture in mind: according to Dana Rotz, as discussed in chapter 2, the *primary* reason why we're seeing less and less divorce is because people are getting married at older ages.[110]

Second, although cohabiting has indeed increased, it actually has been very high for many years. Today, 74 percent of first unions consist of those who live together before or instead of getting married. But twenty years ago, it was already 58 percent. (The majority of the increase came from a very distinct group: those with high school diplomas rather than college degrees.)[111]

And third, most people still get married eventually, so the lower divorce rates are not just because people avoid marriage and live together instead. A Bureau of Labor Statistics (BLS) study shows over 85 percent of couples (90 percent of women) marry by age forty-six.[112] The good news to remember about cohabitation is that at the end of the day, a vast percentage of people will tie the knot.

## Validity of Current Studies (Example of a Big Study Needing a Big Adjustment)

**How can you argue with a heavily documented and highly used government report that says the divorce rate is still about 50 percent?**

In chapter 2, we talked about the CDC report and how it presents the National Survey of Family Growth (NSFG).[113] Both the executive summary within the CDC study itself and all the news reports about it reported that it found a 48 percent divorce rate. Even some of the experts we talked to accept the findings of the CDC/NSFG without question. But there is so much more to the story here and truly a lesson at looking at data closely.

When you compare the CDC/NSFG survey results to the results of one of the main census surveys—the Survey of Income and Program Participation (SIPP)—for the same newlywed period, you see instantly that there is a problem: the CDC divorce rate is *double* that which the census found.

### After Five Years of Marriage

| | |
|---|---|
| 2009 Census Report divorce rate | 10% |
| 2010 CDC/NSFG Report divorce rate | 20% |

We realized the 2009 SIPP survey was more nationally representative for age at marriage and the CDC report was not (as you'll see below). And keep in mind, the first five years of marriage show the highest rate of divorce anyway. So the CDC data was somehow taking a high divorce period in married life and making it look even worse. As with several other similar major discrepancies between surveys we found, we knew this one was worth investigating.

**So why did one report show a divorce rate that was so much worse than the other?**
The bottom line is that both were large surveys, but the CDC report had two major differences: (1) a very large percentage of survey takers were from a much higher-risk group (those married young), and (2) even where the lower-risk people were surveyed, the long-term average didn't include them!

A few details: The CDC report's "average" projected marriage survival rate at twenty years is 52 percent, which would then mean a divorce rate of 48 percent, and that looks *awful*. But once you look closely, you see that average *only* included women who married unusually young. Take a look at this data from the CDC/NSFG (we have put it in a table format that is easier to read, and we added a few words for clarity):

### Marriage Survival Rate of Women Ages 15–44, at Each Anniversary, by Percentage, 2006–2010

| Women | Number in Thousands | 5 years | 10 years | 15 years | 20 years |
|---|---|---|---|---|---|
| Survived | 32,904 | 0.80 | 0.68 | 0.60 | 0.52 |
| **Age at First Marriage** | | | | | |
| Under 20 | 6,874 | 0.70 | 0.54 | 0.46 | 0.37 |
| 20-24 years | 14,166 | 0.81 | 0.69 | 0.60 | 0.55 |
| 25 years and over | 11,863 | 0.86 | 0.78 | 0.73 | N/A |

In this table "N/A" means "not available." Source: Data from CDC/NSFG table 5 (page 16, abbreviated).

Take a look at the twenty-year-anniversary numbers. See that big "not available" under the lowest-risk group of those married at age twenty-five or older? That means that the 52 percent marriage survival average includes *only* the higher-risk groups of those who got married younger than twenty-five! Because this survey only surveyed women up to age forty-four, those who married over age twenty-five hadn't yet had the opportunity to reach their twentieth anniversary.

Since the median age of marriage for women is almost twenty-seven, that supposed average is meaningless for a representative view of marriage and divorce. But that wasn't the purpose of the study anyway; it was studying fertility, so the age forty-four cutoff makes sense for that purpose. Just not to estimate divorce.

**But, really, how far off could these age-at-marriage numbers be from the actual population?**

Pretty far off, actually. In fact, it is almost the *opposite* of the numbers in the actual population! As mentioned, the other reason we can't take the CDC numbers at face value is because the CDC surveyed those married very young, at much higher rates than normal. We put together the table below to show just how skewed the original sample was. We used the Census Bureau 2009 SIPP data to find out what percent of people actually did get married at what ages. As you can see, in the real world (the census data), 76 percent of women get married at age twenty-five or later. But among those in the CDC study (which, again, was designed to study fertility!), 64 percent got married *before* the age of twenty-five!

## Breakdown of Age at First Marriage by Percentage

| Women, Age at First Marriage | Percent of Sample (CDC/NSFG) | Actual Percent in Population (Census) |
|---|---|---|
| Under 20 | 21 | 4.7 |
| 20-24 years | 43 | 19.0 |
| 25 years & over | 36 | 76.3 |
| Total | 100 | 100 |

Source: Data used from the 2006–2010 CDC/NSFG, table 5, and 2009 Census SIPP, table 6 (abbreviated). Total number rounded up from 65.6%.

**Okay, so if this CDC survey had included more representative age groups, what would the divorce-rate numbers have been?** Here's an adjustment that shows how different the results might have been if the age groups were more nationally representative.

### Marriage Survival Rate of Women to Twentieth Anniversary, Weighted by Actual Population

| Women, Age at First Marriage | Percent of Sample (Skewed) CDC/NSFG | Actual Percent in Population Census | Percent of Sample Reaching 20th Anniversary CDC/NSFG | Survival to 20th (Weighted by Actual Size of Each Age Group) |
|---|---|---|---|---|
| Under 20 | 21 | 4.7 | 37 | 2 |
| 20-24 years | 43 | 19.0 | 55 | 10 |
| 25 years & over | 36 | 76.3 | 70 (estimated) | 53 |
| Total | 100 | 100 | | 66 |

Source: Data used from 2006-2010 CDC/NSFG and 2009 Census SIPP (estimated). Total number rounded up from 65.6%.

Even with a very conservative estimate, using more characteristic numbers produces an overall marriage survival rate of 66 percent, meaning an estimated divorce rate of 34 percent.

**Can you explain how you ended up with a 34 percent projected divorce rate?**
Shaunti first looked at three possible ways of predicting what the twentieth anniversary survival rate would be for women twenty-five and older (the number that is "not available" on the CDC/NSFG table). All three methods of adjusting the numbers were

based on other actual trends. She calculated these numbers using conservative estimates, and all delivered similar results of around 70 percent. We felt safe with that number (it could easily be a few points higher).[114]

For the second step, she estimated what the total national average would be *if* ages at marriage were more representative and *with* the new estimated percent of 70 percent of the over-twenty-five age group reaching their twentieth anniversary. We used the "ever divorced" out of "ever married" numbers from the 2009 SIPP (table 6 of their report) to determine the actual age-at-marriage percentages of the total married population. Then we weighted the twentieth-anniversary numbers (now including the 70 percent estimate) by what their percentage *would* have been if the CDC/NSFG numbers resembled the more nationally representative 2009 census numbers. (See table above.)

This process gave us the average of a 66 percent marriage survival rate, thus a 34 percent divorce rate. This number resembles Barna's 2008 survey (33 percent ever divorced) and is only a few points higher than the 2009 SIPP "ever divorced" number of 30.8 percent, so it is very much in the same ballpark. In other words...it's a lot more realistic than the 48 percent divorce rate that should *never* have been reported as a meaningful national average.

**Would this type of reanalysis actually hold up with the experts?**
It depends on what you mean by "hold up." This type of informal adjustment calculation is common when trying to get a handle

on how different certain numbers might be if certain factors were changed.[115] This adjustment would not, as is, hold up to the kind of scrutiny professors have to go through to get a peer-reviewed paper published, proposing that *this* is the new right number. But as you know, our ultimate goal is not to nail down any one final number. And for our bigger-picture purposes, yes, experts have been very interested and supportive.

For example, we e-mailed the adjustments to the CDC/NSFG table to Francesca Adler-Baeder, a professor at Auburn University (and director of the National Stepfamily Resource Center), for feedback. As she put it, "I think you and Shaunti have some interesting questions and are clearly invested in getting the best estimates possible with the best data possible."[116]

Bottom line: always look closely at the actual data because, as the old saying goes, looks can be deceiving.

## What Looks like a 50 Percent Rate

**But what about the census data that shows how few couples reach their fortieth or fiftieth anniversary?**

Table 4 in the 2009 SIPP report that shows anniversaries reached for first marriages, and it looks really depressing at first glance. For women who married in the 1960–64 time frame, only 49.7 percent reached their fortieth wedding anniversary, meaning 50.3 percent didn't! One might think, *There's the proof that half of marriages end in divorce.* Back in the day, we used to assume that too, until we saw a completely different table from the *same survey* that showed how many in roughly the same age group had *actually been divorced*—and it was a much smaller number!

First, take a look at the depressing table on the next page (table 4). Notice the 49.7 percent in the far right column. Yikes!

Now, why is this not the divorce rate?

The first thing to remember is that one main reason for not reaching a golden-years anniversary is not just divorce but death of a spouse! Not surprisingly, since women live longer than men, 60.1 percent of men in that same age group had reached their fortieth wedding anniversary. (And today, this discrepancy in anniversaries becomes even more important in its relevance, since couples are marrying at older ages.)

So how different is the picture when we look *just* at divorce? Another table from the same survey shows us. (See "Female" table 6, "Marital History," on page 149.) It is impossible to do a direct comparison between exactly the same people, unfortunately, since in this next table, the census folks grouped marital history by *age,* not by the year they got married. So we have to extrapolate *a lot,* but it gives us a very different ballpark estimate.

If someone got married in, say, 1964, let's assume (to make it easy) that they were twenty-four years old at the time. That would mean they were born in 1940. So when this census survey was taken in 2009, they would have been sixty-nine years old. Now, look down the column in table 6 for women of that age, and you'll see that only 34.5 percent have ever been divorced![117] Suddenly, the divorce rate doesn't look like 50 percent at all.

Table 4. Percent Reaching Stated Anniversary by Marriage Cohort and Sex, for First Marriages: 2009 (Numbers in Thousands)

| Sex and year of marriage | Number of marriages | Anniversary[1] | | | | | | | |
|---|---|---|---|---|---|---|---|---|---|
| | | 5th | 10th | 15th | 20th | 25th | 30th | 35th | 40th |
| **Men** | | | | | | | | | |
| 1960 to 1964......... | 4,150 | 94.6 | 83.4 | 74.7 | 70.2 | 66.9 | 64.5 | 62.1 | 60.1 |
| 1965 to 1969......... | 5,658 | 91.7 | 80.0 | 69.9 | 65.8 | 62.7 | 60.5 | 57.9 | (X) |
| 1970 to 1974......... | 7,036 | 88.0 | 75.0 | 65.7 | 60.2 | 56.8 | 53.8 | (X) | (X) |
| 1975 to 1979......... | 6,901 | 88.2 | 73.4 | 63.7 | 58.7 | 54.4 | (X) | (X) | (X) |
| 1980 to 1984......... | 7,144 | 90.6 | 74.3 | 65.2 | 60.0 | (X) | (X) | (X) | (X) |
| 1985 to 1989......... | 7,670 | 87.7 | 75.4 | 66.6 | (X) | (X) | (X) | (X) | (X) |
| 1990 to 1994......... | 7,569 | 89.7 | 77.3 | (X) | (X) | (X) | (X) | (X) | (X) |
| 1995 to 1999......... | 8,088 | 89.6 | (X) | (X) | (X) | (X) | (X) | (X) | (X) |
| **Women** | | | | | | | | | |
| 1960 to 1964......... | 5,495 | 93.0 | 82.8 | 73.5 | 67.0 | 60.8 | 57.2 | 53.6 | 49.7 |
| 1965 to 1969......... | 6,705 | 90.7 | 79.3 | 69.6 | 64.0 | 59.1 | 55.8 | 52.1 | (X) |
| 1970 to 1974......... | 7,667 | 89.2 | 74.5 | 66.1 | 61.3 | 56.2 | 52.6 | (X) | (X) |
| 1975 to 1979......... | 7,619 | 86.9 | 72.8 | 63.2 | 57.4 | 53.2 | (X) | (X) | (X) |
| 1980 to 1984......... | 8,051 | 87.8 | 71.1 | 62.9 | 56.6 | (X) | (X) | (X) | (X) |
| 1985 to 1989......... | 8,027 | 87.9 | 74.5 | 66.4 | (X) | (X) | (X) | (X) | (X) |
| 1990 to 1994......... | 8,164 | 87.1 | 74.5 | (X) | (X) | (X) | (X) | (X) | (X) |
| 1995 to 1999......... | 8,229 | 89.5 | (X) | (X) | (X) | (X) | (X) | (X) | (X) |

X Marriage cohort had not all had sufficient time to reach this stated anniversary at the time of this survey.

[1] People reaching stated anniversary.

Source: US Census Bureau, Survey of Income and Program Participation (SIPP), 2008 Panel, Wave 2 Topical Module. For information on sampling and nonsampling error, see www.census.gov/prod/2011pubs/p70-125.pdf.

Table 6. Marital History for People 15 Years and Over by Age and Sex: 2009

| Characteristic | Total, 15 years and over | | 15 to 17 years | 18 to 19 years | 20 to 24 years | 25 to 29 years | 30 to 34 years | 35 to 39 years | 40 to 49 years | 50 to 59 years | 60 to 69 years | 70 years and over |
|---|---|---|---|---|---|---|---|---|---|---|---|---|
| | Estimate | Margin of Error[1] | | | | | | | | | | |
| **FEMALE** | | | | | | | | | | | | |
| Total (in thousands) | 123,272 | 1,022 | 6,259 | 4,219 | 10,158 | 10,408 | 9,645 | 10,267 | 22,119 | 20,702 | 14,288 | 15,207 |
| **Percent** | | | | | | | | | | | | |
| Never married . . . . . | 27.2 | 0.5 | 98.9 | 95.5 | 77.3 | 46.8 | 26.7 | 17.3 | 13.0 | 9.1 | 6.0 | 4.3 |
| Ever married . . . . . . | 72.8 | 0.5 | 1.1 | 4.5 | 22.7 | 53.2 | 73.3 | 82.7 | 87.0 | 90.9 | 94.0 | 95.7 |
| Married once . . . . . | 57.5 | 0.6 | 1.1 | 4.5 | 22.4 | 50.8 | 64.5 | 69.3 | 67.4 | 65.5 | 67.7 | 76.1 |
| Still married[2] . . . | 40.6 | 0.6 | 0.5 | 3.9 | 19.7 | 43.2 | 54.5 | 55.8 | 51.6 | 47.5 | 45.7 | 30.1 |
| Married twice . . . . | 12.1 | 0.4 | 0.1 | – | 0.3 | 2.3 | 8.0 | 11.6 | 15.8 | 19.5 | 20.1 | 15.2 |
| Still married[2] . . . | 7.9 | 0.3 | 1.0 | – | 0.2 | 2.0 | 6.9 | 9.1 | 11.3 | 13.4 | 13.2 | 5.2 |
| Married 3 or more times . . . . . . . | 3.2 | 0.2 | – | – | – | – | 0.8 | 1.9 | 3.8 | 5.9 | 6.2 | 4.4 |
| Still married[2] . . . | 1.9 | 0.2 | – | – | – | – | 0.7 | 1.4 | 2.5 | 4.1 | 3.6 | 1.4 |
| Ever divorced . . . . . | 22.4 | 0.5 | 0.2 | 0.2 | 1.8 | 7.3 | 15.6 | 22.7 | 31.0 | 37.3 | 34.5 | 21.4 |
| Currently divorced | 11.3 | 0.4 | 0.1 | 0.2 | 1.5 | 5.3 | 8.1 | 11.8 | 16.4 | 18.6 | 16.0 | 9.9 |
| Ever widowed . . . . | 10.0 | 0.4 | 0.4 | 0.2 | 0.1 | 0.2 | 0.6 | 1.4 | 2.6 | 6.5 | 17.0 | 51.2 |
| Currently widowed | 8.9 | 0.3 | 0.4 | 0.2 | 0.1 | 0.1 | 0.4 | 0.8 | 1.8 | 4.9 | 13.9 | 48.3 |

(continued on next page)

Table 6. Marital History for People 15 Years and Over by Age and Sex: 2009 (continued)

| Characteristic | Total, 15 years and over | | 15 to 17 years | 18 to 19 years | 20 to 24 years | 25 to 29 years | 30 to 34 years | 35 to 39 years | 40 to 49 years | 50 to 59 years | 60 to 69 years | 70 years and over |
| | Estimate | Margin of Error[1] | | | | | | | | | | |
|---|---|---|---|---|---|---|---|---|---|---|---|---|
| Total (in thousands) | 115,797 | 1,024 | 6,559 | 4,311 | 10,152 | 10,567 | 9,518 | 9,995 | 21,504 | 19,568 | 12,774 | 10,849 |
| **MALE** | | | | | | | | | | | | |
| Percent | | | | | | | | | | | | |
| Never married ..... | 33.0 | 0.6 | 98.3 | 97.5 | 87.5 | 59.7 | 35.6 | 23.5 | 16.4 | 10.8 | 4.6 | 3.4 |
| Ever married....... | 67.0 | 0.6 | 1.7 | 2.5 | 12.5 | 40.3 | 64.4 | 76.5 | 83.6 | 89.2 | 95.4 | 96.6 |
| Married once...... | 52.3 | 0.6 | 1.5 | 2.5 | 12.5 | 38.8 | 59.4 | 66.9 | 65.8 | 63.4 | 64.8 | 72.3 |
| Still married[2] ... | 42.5 | 0.6 | 1.0 | 1.8 | 11.2 | 34.2 | 52.2 | 56.1 | 52.2 | 50.4 | 53.5 | 54.0 |
| Married twice ..... | 11.6 | 0.4 | 0.2 | - | - | 1.5 | 4.8 | 8.7 | 14.8 | 20.0 | 22.1 | 18.9 |
| Still married[2] ... | 9.0 | 0.4 | 0.1 | - | - | 1.3 | 4.0 | 7.4 | 11.3 | 15.5 | 17.5 | 13.2 |
| Married 3 or more times....... | 3.1 | 0.2 | - | - | - | 0.1 | 0.2 | 1.0 | 3.0 | 5.8 | 8.5 | 5.4 |
| Still married[2] ... | 2.3 | 0.2 | - | - | - | 0.1 | 0.2 | 0.8 | 2.2 | 4.3 | 6.5 | 3.8 |
| Ever divorced...... | 20.5 | 0.5 | 0.4 | 0.1 | 0.8 | 5.0 | 10.5 | 17.9 | 28.5 | 35.7 | 36.5 | 23.4 |
| Currently divorced | 9.1 | 0.4 | 0.3 | 0.1 | 0.7 | 3.7 | 6.2 | 9.5 | 14.2 | 15.5 | 12.4 | 7.2 |
| Ever widowed .... | 3.6 | 0.2 | 0.3 | 0.5 | 0.1 | 0.3 | 0.2 | 0.5 | 1.3 | 2.5 | 6.4 | 22.6 |
| Currently widowed | 2.6 | 0.2 | 0.2 | 0.5 | 0.1 | 0.3 | 0.1 | 0.3 | 0.9 | 1.6 | 3.9 | 17.4 |

- Represents or rounds to zero.

[1] This number, then added to and subtracted from the estimate, provides the 90 percent confidence interval.

[2] Includes those currently separated.

Source: US Census Bureau, Survey of Income and Program Participation (SIPP), 2008 Panel, Wave 2 Topical Module. For information on sampling and nonsampling error, see www.census.gov/prod/2011pubs/p70-125.pdf.

**What about college textbooks saying divorce remains at 50 percent?**

This has come up in conversations Shaunti has had with many pastors, therapists, and others who work in the marriage arena who have been assuming that textbooks are the most likely sources of good data. But after doing some research, we learned that while textbooks can indeed be helpful for a good overview of various factors, they are not necessarily the most up-to-date or thorough resource. In fact, we were taken aback at how often a 50 percent divorce rate is stated as fact in textbooks, without making clear that those were projections, not measurements—and without mentioning that the current "ever divorced" number is much, much better.

The late Norval Glenn, who was a highly revered marriage researcher and sociologist, penned a harsh critique about college textbooks on the subject of marriage and divorce. He stated in *Closed Hearts, Closed Minds: The Textbook Story of Marriage,* "Current textbooks convey a determinedly pessimistic view of marriage. Both by what they say and, sometimes even more importantly, by the information they omit, these books repeatedly suggest that marriage is more a problem than a solution." He also emphasized that "these books are typically riddled with glaring errors, distortions of research, omissions of important data, and misattributions of scholarship."[118]

However, we were delighted to find one highly respected expert who is actually a marriage champion (not a detractor) and is also currently in the process of revising his textbook. We spoke

with Dr. David Olson who, besides directing his PREPARE/
ENRICH organization, is an author of a college sociology textbook. Dr. Olson agreed that there was room to revise projections
down from 50 percent and that projecting a "40 to 50 percent
divorce rate is now more accurate."[119] Of course, as you know, we
think it is also important for people to be aware that the current
prevalence of divorce has not reached that range.

### But aren't there a lot of divorced baby boomers who could drive the divorce rate up?

In short: yes, the baby boomers have the greatest divorce risk, but
it looks like the risk is more relevant for second marriages than
first ones. Unfortunately, the press isn't really making that dis-
tinction clear in all the articles about it. "The Gray Divorce Revolution" is one newer and highly publicized study about divorce
among those over fifty.[120] At first glance, this study looks like a
bad-news study that might refute the idea that divorce will continue to decline, because it shows an increase in baby boomer
divorces between 1990 and 2010. But, once we looked closer, the
numbers actually revealed better news than ever expected. Nearly
70 percent of those fifty and over are still married and in their
first marriage...very similar to what the Census 2009 SIPP data
found for everyone else!

Plus, some believe the survey used here, the American Community Survey (ACS), might overestimate divorce and should
not (as this study does) be compared to a completely different
data set—in this case, actual vital statistics.[121]

Yes, the findings on divorce in remarriages were not as positive, as the "Gray Divorce" study indicated a higher number of remarriages (and some short-lived first and second marriages) that end in divorce. However, as stated in chapter 5, the most recent study on remarriages ending by divorce, by the Bureau of Labor Statistics (BLS), found the youngest baby boomers experienced redivorce at a rate of only 36 percent.[122]

## Projections of a 50 Percent Rate

**Haven't *many* experts said divorce would eventually reach 50 percent?**
Yes, many experts over the years have projected the divorce rate will hit 50 percent or higher. But again, the key word here is *projection.* Except for some of the very highest-risk groups (such as those married as a teenager), the actual "ever divorced" divorce rate has not hit that, even after many decades of marriage.

Dr. Larry Bumpass, though retired, is still considered one of the preeminent experts in this field. But his projections used older data, largely during the years when divorce was still especially high. For instance, using the 1985 Current Population Survey (CPS), Dr. Bumpass projected a 56 percent divorce rate by forty years of marriage and a possible lifetime estimate of a two-thirds disruption rate.[123] That would mean only about 33 percent of first marriages would actually survive! But in terms of what has actually happened, as you'll remember, the Census 2009 SIPP shows that 72 percent of first marriages are still intact, and the numbers are similar even among some of the highest-risk baby boomer groups.

Dr. Robert Schoen is another authority in the demography arena, and he used different data in the past, including vital statistics and the 1995 CPS to reach an estimate of an approximately 43 percent marriage-ending rate.[124] And yet, as another expert—Dr. Amato—reminded us (see chapter 2), Schoen's data *did not distinguish* whether a marriage was a first marriage or not, or, more importantly, if it ended in death or divorce.[125]

**But are the experts today, such as Dr. Amato and others, still projecting a 40 to 50 percent rate?**

Yes, they are. Consistently.[126] And as we said, they are the experts and time may prove them right. But there's an important behind-the-scenes observation worth noting. Among nearly all the elite researchers we have spoken with, there is clearly a reluctance to go too far "out on a limb" (as several put it), in projecting something lower than that 40 to 50 percent rate. Not because their calculations couldn't deliver a different number (remember, projections are based on assumptions), but because that is the consensus range of the research community. Two of these researchers cautioned Shaunti that speculating about a projected divorce rate lower than that barrier of 40 percent would risk the credibility of the book because it would fall outside the perceived norm.

However, we are not alone in wondering about these projections. Glenn Stanton at Focus on the Family is another analyst who has been working to bring the good news about marriage into the public awareness. He has also questioned whether the experts' projections sufficiently reflect the positive trends. As he told Shaunti,

> Bumpass has done amazing work, even though it is older now. The problem is, to some degree we all tend to assume that the things that get cited by good people are timeless and not changing. But circumstances do change, and our understanding changes. We hopefully are learning new things all the time. So we probably should be willing to take a look at it. We should absolutely be willing to ask, "What can we know and not know from the 1995 data Bumpass used, and where should we not have relied on that, when the Census Bureau has recent stuff?" Some of the experts have told me, "That's the best data we have," and the question we need to ask is, "How reliable is the best data we have?" There's a lot of work to do on clearing up misconceptions, and we need good data to do it.[127]

The weight of evidence suggests that it might be reasonable to adjust the assumptions for some of the more positive trends and see if there are alternative projections worth discussing. That was one reason we were so grateful for Dr. Amato's willingness to speculate out loud that the divorce rate could in fact be lower than 40 percent, perhaps 35 percent or some other number.

## Remarriage and Redivorce

**If all these leaders say second marriages have a 60 percent divorce rate and third marriages have a 73 percent chance of divorce, then does it matter if an actual study can't be found?**

It matters a lot, precisely *because* those same experts could not point us to an actual study. As we said in chapter 5, the Census Bureau is often cited as the source of these percentages, but they have no record of these numbers. We contacted several experts who have these numbers on their websites, and they could not point us to any actual study that substantiates these percentages.

We recognize that Dr. Bumpass, along with Kelly Raley, Dr. Andrew Cherlin, and Dr. Mavis Hetherington, projected higher divorce rates in remarriages in the past. For instance, Andrew Cherlin said in one of his books that he estimates 37 percent of remarriages will end in divorce within ten years of marriage, compared to 30 percent of first marriages.[128] He based his estimate on data by Larry Bumpass, which stemmed from surveys in the 1980s. (Incidentally, Dr. Cherlin's book is already, as of this writing, twenty-two years old.) In light of the most recent BLS study indicating only 36 percent of second marriages of high-risk baby boomers have ended and the fact that no one so far has reproduced the actual quoted census study (or any others) that show an actual 60 percent and 73 percent divorce rate for higher-order marriages, those high numbers seem highly unlikely to be accurate.

Because Dr. Cherlin was on sabbatical in 2013 while we were writing this book, he explained that he was unable to be interviewed due to the timing. We heard his name most often about this research, and he seems like the best candidate to put his hands on these numbers, if the study is out there.

**I looked in the census tables and I don't see a table for "marriages still intact" for first marriages or remarriages. Can you explain how you got your numbers?**

The numbers have to be calculated from the Census 2009 SIPP. Officially, the report is called "Number, Timing, and Duration of Marriages and Divorces: 2009." Table 6 of the SIPP report (the "Marital History" table on pages 149–150) details all the marriage information and data. The table below summarizes how you do the calculations for men and women individually:

|  | Men | Women |
| --- | --- | --- |
| Married once | 52.3% | 57.5% |
| Still married | 42.5% | 40.6% |
| Still in 1st marriage | 42.5/52.3 = 81.2% | 40.6/57.5 = 70.6% |
| Married twice | 11.6% | 12.1% |
| Still married | 9.0% | 7.9% |
| Still in 2nd marriage | 9.0/11.6 = 77.6% | 7.9/12.1 = 65.3% |
| Married 3+ times* | 3.1% | 3.2% |
| Still married | 2.3% | 1.9% |
| Still in 3rd marriage | 2.3/3.1 = 74.2% | 1.9/3.2 = 59.4% |

*Includes those married three or more times.

**Isn't that third-marriage dissolution rate for women still pretty high?**

Actually, for both women and men in third marriages, the odds are highly probable the dissolution results from death, not divorce.

They are presumably significantly older at the beginning of their marital unions. Since women tend to live longer than men, one would expect a difference in all their percentages if the main reason is widowhood, which is exactly what we see. Moreover, table 6 of the SIPP report lists widowhood; currently widowed men are at 2.6 percent, compared to women at 8.9 percent currently widowed.

**Your calculations show a higher number for men still in first marriage and a slightly lower one for women. How did you get an overall 72 percent first-marriage rate, then?**

There's a SIPP table (table 10 on the next page) that actually shows the overall number for *couples,* not just men or women.

Both spouses married only one time and still married is 71.5 percent, which the Census Bureau rounds up to 72 percent. This table also shows the breakdown by percentage of second and third or more marriages.

## More Studies About the Impact of Faith

**You mentioned other studies about the impact of religion/faith on marriage. Can you provide some examples?**

Yes, there are so many studies we could not give them all their due credit. Below we list a few that we found relevant and significant to our research.

a. The CDC/NSFG 2002 report found the importance of religion to lower divorce rates. As we already pointed out in this

## Table 10. Number of Times Married for Currently Married Wives and Their Husbands: 2009 (Numbers in Thousands)

| Number of times wife has been married | Number of times husband has been married | | | | | | | |
|---|---|---|---|---|---|---|---|---|
| | All current marriages | | | | Married within the last year[1] | | | |
| | Total | Married 1 time | Married 2 times | Married 3 or more times | Total | Married 1 time | Married 2 times | Married 3 or more times |
| Total........... | 60,607 | 47,699 | 10,271 | 2,637 | 2,232 | 1,648 | 440 | 144 |
| Married 1 time........... | 48,779 | 43,340 | 4,705 | 734 | 1,696 | 1,447 | 224 | 24 |
| Married 2 times........... | 9,551 | 3,814 | 4,533 | 1,205 | 422 | 163 | 167 | 92 |
| Married 3 or more times ... | 2,276 | 545 | 1,034 | 698 | 114 | 37 | 50 | 27 |
| **PERCENT OF MARRIAGES** | | | | | | | | |
| Total........... | 100.0 | 78.7 | 16.9 | 4.4 | 100.0 | 73.8 | 19.7 | 6.4 |
| Married 1 time........... | 80.5 | 71.5 | 7.8 | 1.2 | 76.0 | 64.9 | 10.0 | 1.1 |
| Married 2 times........... | 15.8 | 6.3 | 7.5 | 2.0 | 18.9 | 7.3 | 7.5 | 4.1 |
| Married 3 or more times ... | 3.8 | 0.9 | 1.7 | 1.2 | 5.1 | 1.7 | 2.2 | 1.2 |

[1] Includes marriages that occurred during calendar year 2008.

Note: This table includes only people who are married, spouse present.

Source: US Census Bureau, Survey of Income and Program Participation (SIPP), 2008 Panel, Wave 2 Topical Module. For information on sampling and nonsampling error, see www.census.gov/prod/2011pubs/p70-125.pdf.

section, that survey is skewed on divorce-rate projections overall. However, *within* the survey, the difference between religious and non-religious survey takers is still helpful. Those who said faith was "very important" to them had a 28 percent lower divorce rate within fifteen years compared to those who said it was "not important."[129]

b. Dr. W. Bradley Wilcox, mentioned several times in the book already, is well known in the academic world for his marriage research. Besides being a sociology professor at the University of Virginia and director of the National Marriage Project, Brad is also principal investigator (along with collaborator Jeffrey Dew) for the Survey of Marital Generosity. This survey, among other things, shows a roughly 70 percent drop in how likely the couples *think* they are to divorce, among couples where both partners attended church regularly, compared to those where both partners didn't.[130]

c. Dr. Bradley Wright of the University of Connecticut studied the General Social Survey (GSS) for his 2010 book *Christians Are Hate-Filled Hypocrites...and Other Lies You've Been Told*. He found that evangelicals who attended church weekly decreased their rate of divorce by 22 percent over those evangelicals who never attended. The GSS is conducted regularly by the National Opinion Research Center at the University of Chicago and goes beyond attendance and affiliation, by asking questions about religious activities, prayer, and if the survey takers "feel guided by God in daily activities."[131]

d. Dr. Annette Mahoney of Bowling Green State University

leads the way in academic research looking at the impact of religion on families. In one key project, she published a review of 184 peer-reviewed studies and summarized that, overall, "the findings imply that higher general religiousness helps form (e.g., marital unions) and maintain (e.g., lowers divorce risk) traditional family bonds." In another study, Mahoney calculated and found a 13 percent decrease in the divorce rate in people with a specific religious identification compared to those with none. When it came to religious attendance, she calculated a 16 percent lower divorce rate with those who went to church regularly compared to those who didn't attend on a regular basis.[132]

e. The FamilyLife Family Needs Survey, mentioned before, found that those who prayed or read the Bible together in any kind of a regular way, even just a few times a month, cut their marital danger signals in half.[133] FamilyLife uses a sophisticated "Marital/Relational Health Assessment" to analyze whether a relationship seems quite healthy, moderate with some concern, or high risk, and uses the traffic light analogy of green, yellow, and red to indicate each. Among those who prayed together sometimes, only 7 percent had a lot of "red" danger signals, compared to 14 percent among those who rarely or never prayed together. They also found that 69 percent of those who prayed together sometimes were in the healthy "green" category, compared to 56 percent among those who rarely or never prayed together. There was, however, very little reduction in the various rates of past divorce based on the prayer and Bible reading categories.[134]

## Other Ways to Get Data

**How can I access some of these numbers and information for my talks, sermons, school papers, or other uses?**

Within the individual sources we cite, you'll find a lot of good data tables (tables of census data, for example). At our website, www.goodnewsmarriage.com, we have a crib sheet of websites we found helpful and used for the book.

**If I don't have time to look on your website, can you point me to one good resource?**

A good place to start is the Institute for Family Studies (IFS). Scott Stanley and Brad Wilcox are senior fellows for this relatively new resource that highlights the latest in marriage research. Their blog even includes ready-to-tweet quotes. The IFS website can be accessed at http://ifstudies.org.

# Acknowledgments

After Tally and I first learned the divorce rate wasn't what we thought it was, we set out to discover the truth—with no idea we were initiating a project that would take eight years, thousands of hours, and the help of hundreds of generous people. Although there is no way to list every name, we want everyone to know we deeply appreciate your help. Please forgive us if our tired brains inadvertently left anyone out. Thank you to...

The many renowned demographers, sociologists, and other experts who have been working in this field for years, who advised, informed, and provided us excellent and often customized data through meetings, conference calls, and e-mails. Most especially we thank Dr. Scott Stanley at the University of Denver, Dr. Brad Wilcox at the University of Virginia, Dr. Sam Sturgeon at Demographic Intelligence, Dr. Jeffrey Dew at Utah State University, director Tom Smith at the General Social Survey, and the incredibly skilled and helpful staff of the US Census Bureau ACS and SIPP offices (who, due to policy, preferred not be named). Our thanks also to Dr. Paul Amato at Penn State University, Dr. Dana Rotz at Mathematica Policy Research, Dr. Linda Waite at the University of Chicago, Dr. David Olson at PREPARE/ENRICH, Dr. Steven Beach at the University of

Georgia, Dr. Kelly Raley at the University of Texas, Dr. Betsey Stevenson at the University of Michigan, Dr. Annette Mahoney at Bowling Green State University, Dr. Christopher Ellison at the University of Texas–San Antonio, Dr. Tim Heaton at Brigham Young University, Dr. Sheela Kennedy at the University of Minnesota, Dr. Bradley Wright at the University of Connecticut, Dr. Francesca Adler-Baeder and Dr. Chelsea Garneau at Auburn University. Our thanks also to Dr. Andrew Cherlin at Johns Hopkins University; though he was on sabbatical and not directly interviewed, we heavily drew upon his work.

Clint Jenkin and Pam Jacob at Barna Group, who worked with us many months to dig out the real answers about churchgoers, George Barna for his leadership in the research arena over so many years, and David Kinnaman for his leadership of Barna Group today.

Dr. Chuck Cowan at Analytic Focus and Felicia Rogers and the team at Decision Analyst for their expert help and support of my own research surveys over the years, including those in this book. Thanks also to Matthew St. John of the Knights of Columbus for providing valuable information from their commissioned Marist Poll.

Other leading experts and analysts in the marriage arena from a policy, research, therapy, and ministry perspective, who helped us in so many ways. We are especially indebted to the team at FamilyLife, particularly Family Needs Survey director Glenn Gritzon, Greg Weaver, Ron Deal, Chuck Eckerson, Bill Eyster, Bob Lepine, and Dennis Rainey, as well as Dr. Peter Larson at Tango Group. Our thanks also to Jim Daly and the leaders at Focus on the Family, especially Glenn Stanton. Many others provided information, counsel, and feedback during the process, including Pat Fagan at Family Research Council, Ed Stetzer, Dwayne Ewers and John Wilke at LifeWay Research, Dr. John Trent, Dr. Wendy Walsh, Diane Mannina at Heritage Foundation, as well as Randy Hicks and Jamie Lord with the Georgia Center for Opportunity, who first helped me understand the basics. We are very grateful to Jim Burns at HomeWord for seeing the potential in this information and encouraging us to share it, and also to Ted Lowe at MarriedPeople, Tyler Reagin at Catalyst, and other leaders for giving us the opportunity to do so.

The dozens of pastors, priests, marriage therapists, psychologists, social workers, counselors, coaches, church leaders, and other faith clergy who answered my call, took meetings, and gave me invaluable insight and perspective, especially Andy Stanley, pastor of North Point Community Church, who wrote the foreword and whose encouragement was invaluable for initially launching me into marriage ministry; and the North Point staff team, especially Diane Grant, Erica McCurdy, Debbie Causey, and Tricia Sherriff, and the counseling team that provided such important input.

The amazing team at WaterBrook Multnomah, especially Dave Kopp, who has been encouraging me in this research for years, our wonderful editor Susan Tjaden, and Ken Petersen, Steve Cobb, Carie Freimuth, Lori Addicott, Allison O'Hara, Laura Wright, Karen Sherry, and Julia Wallace.

While the professional help of those above was vital, we could never have completed the course without the unswerving support, love, and encouragement from our most important people.

*From Tally:* I am indebted to Shaunti for this unbelievable opportunity and for the last eight years; to Bob Hostetler, who originally recommended me to Shaunti; and to my church, small group, book club, and countless friends, family, and loved ones who supported me during this process. And finally, to my husband, Eric, and our four precious kids, who remind me daily about the good news in marriage. Thanks be to God!

*From Shaunti:* I am so amazed and grateful for the skill and passion of Tally Whitehead, who started as a research assistant and turned into a true partner in this work. I'm thankful for my tremendous staff, especially my staff director, Linda Crews, and past and present team members Theresa Colquitt, Kathy Dunmon, Debbie Licona, Cathy Kidd, and Karen Newby, who found themselves running the whole show the last year or two as I disappeared under the weight of *four* book deadlines. Also Naomi Duncan, Julie Fidler, Jenny Reynolds, and the many others I have depended on in so many ways.

I deeply appreciate my parents, Dick and Judy Reidinger, as well as Calvin Edwards, Lisa and Eric Rice, my amazing prayer team, and so many other friends for their constant encouragement and practical help.

Most important, none of this would have happened were it not for my wonderful husband, Jeff, and our children, who not only carried me every step of the way, but who showed me the love of God every day. Ultimately it is His love and guidance that kept pulling me and Tally forward and brought this book into existence, and I thank Him most of all.

# Notes

1. Ann Patchett, "Ann Patchett Tells Everything She Knows About Love," *Reader's Digest,* November 2013, www.rd.com /true-stories/love/ann-patchett-tells-everything-she-knows -about-love.
2. Wendy D. Manning, Susan L. Brown, and Krista K. Payne, "Two Decades of Stability and Change in Age at First Union Formation," Working Paper Series WP-13-06, National Center for Family and Marriage Research (Bowling Green State University, October 2013), 22, www.bgsu.edu/content/dam /BGSU/college-of-arts-and-sciences/NCFMR/documents/WP /Wp-13-06.pdf.
3. Joyce A. Martin et al., "Births: Final Data for 2011," *National Vital Statistics Reports* 62, no. 1 (June 2013): 9, table C, www .cdc.gov/nchs/data/nvsr/nvsr62/nvsr62_01.pdf.
4. The words "divorce rate" can mean many different things. In this book, wherever I don't otherwise state the type of divorce rate, I will be referring to the society-wide divorce rate as commonly understood by most people I interview: the percentage of marriages that have ended in divorce. Throughout this book, I refer to it as the "prevalence of divorce," the "current divorce rate," or just the "divorce rate." Wherever I discuss a different type of divorce rate—for example, a projection of new marriages that might end in divorce, the crude divorce rate, various divorce-ratio models, and so on—I will make clear which type of divorce rate I am referencing.

5. Sixty million is a rough middle of the road. According to the American Community Survey 2012, there are approximately 63.7 million current marriages; when respondents were asked if their spouse was present, the number drops to about 57.8 million marriages. See US Census Bureau, 2012 American Community Survey, "Sex by Marital Status for the Population 15 Years and Over," http://factfinder2.census.gov/faces/table services/jsf/pages/productview.xhtml?pid=ACS_12_1YR _B12001&prodType=table.

6. But remember, the expert I first talked to said (see opening of chapter 1), no one actually knows what the real divorce rate is—not just because there are many different types of divorce rates, but because the government discontinued collection of actual divorce certificate data for vital statistics in the late 1990s and has relied on survey samples since then.

7. Rose M. Kreider and Renee Ellis, "Number, Timing, and Duration of Marriages and Divorces: 2009," *Current Population Reports* P70-125 (May 2011): 19, table 10, www.census.gov/prod /2011pubs/p70-125.pdf. This report is drawn from the Census Bureau's 2009 Survey of Income and Program Participation, popularly referred to in the industry as SIPP. Although there are other surveys that have begun to be fielded in recent years, the SIPP remains a standard that numerous experts refer to regularly. Many experts have high hopes for the American Community Survey, but because it is a brand-new type of annual survey, it will be years before it will show us any meaningful, long-term trends.

8. Data for 2001 shows 70 percent of both spouses are in first marriages in Rose M. Kreider, "Number, Timing, and Duration of Marriages and Divorces: 2001," *Current Population Reports* P70-97 (February 2005): 12, table 8, www.census.gov/prod /2005pubs/p70-97.pdf. Data for 1996 shows more than 70 percent of both spouses are in first marriages in Rose M. Kreider and Jason M. Fields, "Number, Timing, and Duration

of Marriages and Divorces: 1996," *Current Population Reports* P70-80 (February 2002): 19, www.census.gov/prod/2002pubs/ p70-80.pdf.

9. Arthur J. Norton and Louisa F. Miller, "Remarriage Among Women in the United States: 1985," *Current Population Reports* P-23, no. 169 (December 1990), www.census.gov /hhes/socdemo/marriage/data/cps/P23.169.1990.Report1 .pdf. In this report, they delineated divorce and widowhood rates; the actual divorce rate for first marriages in 1985 was 23.1 percent. (This is calculated from page 2, table A: divorced after first marriage/ever married 17,142/73,971 = 23.17.) That means approximately 76.9 percent were either still married or widowed. Subtracting out those widowed will probably bring the number down to roughly at or below the 72 percent rate of today. Note that the 1975 and 1985 surveys are a different type of survey from the 1996, 2001, and 2009 SIPP surveys.

10. Links to the 1996, 2001, and 2009 SIPP (and the technical citation information) can be found at www.census.gov/hhes /socdemo/marriage/data/sipp/index.html.

11. Glenn Gritzon, "Super Composite for 2012–2013 of the Family Needs Survey Findings," FamilyLife, Little Rock, AR, 2013, www.familylife.com/FNS.

12. Although this is simply a rough estimate—since it applies the rate of widowhood from a completely different data set to the Census Bureau data—the end number of 20 percent may be a bit conservative. The eight-point drop due to widowhood was found in surveys that were primarily among churchgoers, who analytically are less likely to have various health-risk factors (such as smoking) that lead to mortality at younger ages. Thus, among the general population, the rate of widowhood could potentially be even greater than the eight percentage points found in the church population; so the actual first-marriage divorce rate could be lower than 20 percent.

13. There are multiple other well-researched studies that have found different ratios that, for various reasons, are not good nationally representative averages for the total population. For example, a 2009 study, "The Marriage Index," from the Institute for American Values—led by an excellent team of researchers— shows in the table "Marriage Index: Monitoring the Nation's Leading Marriage Indicators" that only 61.2 percent of first marriages are intact, which on the surface could imply a quite high 38.8 divorce rate. But in addition to not knowing which marriages ended in death rather than divorce, this particular survey only sampled those between the ages of twenty and fifty-nine. In other words, it included the worst divorce years of those aged fifty to fifty-nine years (the baby boomer generation has the highest divorce rate) and didn't include the better data from the older women. (See www.americanvalues.org/search /item.php?id=44.)

14. As with many of these surveys, getting the correct "ever divorced" number took a bit of calculating. On the Census Bureau's "Marital History for People 15 Years Old and Over by Age and Sex: 2009" (Kreider and Ellis, "Number, Timing, and Duration: 2009," 16, table 6), the percent of women "ever divorced" is just 22.4 percent. But that is *of the total female population* surveyed (123,272 women) and not of women ever married (which was 89,742). Calculating 22.4 percent of the total population delivers the number 27,613, which, when divided by women ever married, brings the real ratio of those ever divorced to 30.8 percent.

15. Kreider and Ellis, "Number, Timing, and Duration: 2009," 16, table 6 (derived percentage as noted above).

16. The final 2012 "ever divorced" number was provided directly in personal correspondence with Tom Smith, November 20, 2013. For general survey information, Tom W. Smith et al. "General Social Surveys, 1972–2012," National Opinion Research

Center, University of Chicago, March 2013, http://www3.norc
.org/GSS+Website.

17. Norval D. Glenn, "With This Ring: A National Survey on
Marriage in America," National Fatherhood Initiative, 2005,
32, http://blog.fatherhood.org/with-this-ring-survey. (The
survey was conducted 2003–2004.)

18. Barna Group, "New Marriage and Divorce Statistics Released,"
March 31, 2008, www.barna.org/barna-update/family-kids
/42-new-marriage-and-divorce-statistics-released#.UnfR8
-Ao6Uk.

19. Knights of Columbus / Marist Poll Survey, 2010. Poll data
first appeared in Carl Anderson, *Beyond a House Divided: The
Moral Consensus Ignored by Washington, Wall Street, and the
Media* (New York: Doubleday, 2010), 101. Poll data was
provided to authors by Knights of Columbus via e-mail, April
18, 2013.

20. Kreider and Ellis, "Number, Timing, and Duration: 2009," 16,
table 6, the birth cohort among women ages sixty to sixty-nine.
Note that among the fifty to fifty-nine age cohort, the percent
ever divorced was calculated as 41 percent. But that too gives a
misleading picture. See the FAQ section for more on the "gray
divorce" issue among baby boomers.

21. Beyond the "ever divorced" method discussed here, the Census
Bureau has also attempted a completely different way of
looking at and trying to estimate the divorce rate, as shown in
figure 5 ("Cumulative Percentage of Ever-Married Women
Divorced from First Marriage by Race and Ethnicity and
Duration of First Marriage: 2009") in the SIPP report
(Kreider and Ellis, "Number, Timing, and Duration: 2009,"
15). This method delivers a cumulative estimate that roughly
40 percent of first-time marriages have ended in divorce by
forty years of marriage. However, in our judgment, the
complex cumulative methodology used on the data provided

by survey takers delivers a result that contradicts the actual "ever divorced" numbers for *those same people,* shown in SIPP table 6. Table 6 shows a significantly lower divorce rate average for those survey takers who could have (by age) reached a fortieth anniversary. (Combining the age groups of those sixty and above, only 29 percent had ever been divorced, and even adding in a few younger boomers who got married young wouldn't change that percentage much.) In a November 14, 2013, conversation, the Census Bureau official who did the full SIPP report explained that figure 5 was an alternative way to try to get a handle on these complex divorce numbers. However, because the calculations for this method were not published, we were unable to examine them. (As far as we can tell, this cumulative method has not been widely used by the demographers and sociologists who work in this field.) The official also explained that figure 5 was not primarily used to estimate the divorce rate but to show the difference in divorce between racial groups. Bottom line, while this cumulative method might be helpful to show the differences in divorce between racial groups, it does not appear to deliver a number consistent with the actual "ever divorced" numbers published in table 6.

22. Among most experts, this fact is uncontested. However, a recent working paper by Dr. Sheela Kennedy and Dr. Steven Ruggles of the University of Minnesota theorized that because of widespread reporting problems (see next footnote), the divorce rate may not actually be continuing to drop. But whether or not the earlier trend has plateaued, the divorce rate is certainly far down from its peak. We have added a discussion on this in the FAQ section of the book.

See Sheela Kennedy and Steven Ruggles, "Breaking Up Is Hard to Count: The Rise of Divorce and Cohabitation Instability in the United States, 1980–2010" (working paper

2013-01, Minnesota Population Center, University of Minnesota, Minneapolis, April 2013), www.pop.umn.edu/sites/www.pop.umn.edu/files/WorkingPaper_Breaking_Up_April2013.pdf.

23. Even this number of reported divorces is fraught with problems, since there is such a wide swing in the consistency of reporting of the number of divorces at the local, regional, and state level from year to year. For example, a given city hall might report divorces one year and not the next, and that happens all over the country. But in aggregate, it is still the only number that has been tracked for years that gives us anything like a trend from the same sources, year after year, without changing how the number is calculated.

24. A related way of looking at this trend is the "refined divorce rate," which is the number of divorces per one thousand married women (rather than per one thousand people). The refined divorce rate should be more meaningful because it compares divorces to those married, but unfortunately we haven't found any source that has used the same data set for "number of married women" from the 1960s through today. So comparing the numbers would mean you were looking at one type of number in this decade and another type of number in a different decade, thereby meaning it's not a true trend. Several researchers have switched to using the American Community Survey (ACS), which added a question about divorce in 2008. This will eventually give us great data but at the moment is not helpful for a trend, especially when trying to compare today's divorce rate to the divorce rate peak in the 1979 to 1981 period. However, we can estimate the refined divorce rate using a chart created by sociologist Bradley Wright (obtained by personal e-mail); he calculates that the refined divorce rate in 2009 was 16.4. In other words, roughly sixteen married women out of every thousand got divorced that year. That refined divorce rate

number peaked at 22.8 in 1979 and has been steadily falling ever since, declining more than 28 percent overall; it is therefore in the same ballpark as the crude divorce rate drop of 32 percent.

25. US Census Bureau, "Births, Deaths, Marriages, and Divorces," *Statistical Abstract of the United States: 2012,* 65, table 78, www .census.gov/prod/2011pubs/12statab/vitstat.pdf. For crude divorce rates from 2000–2011: Centers for Disease Control and Prevention, National Center for Health Statistics, "National Marriage and Divorce Rate Trends: Provisional Number of Marriages and Marriage Rate: United States 2000–2011," www.cdc.gov/nchs/nvss/marriage_divorce_tables.htm.

26. Manning, Brown, and Payne, "Two Decades," 22.

27. Manning, Brown, and Payne, "Two Decades," 6.

28. Scott M. Stanley, Galena K. Rhoades, and Howard J. Markman, "Sliding vs. Deciding: Inertia and the Premarital Cohabitation Effect," *Family Relations* 55 (2006): 499–509, https:// app.box.com/s/59fd9e71728ef08658be. This study found that couples who were living together without being officially engaged were more likely to divorce if they did get married. In general, various negative results in the relationship when couples live together before marriage (especially before getting engaged) are well documented and known as the cohabitation effect. Dr. Stanley and others have found, for example, that these couples experience a higher risk of divorce later, as well as depression and domestic aggression. Couples who cohabit also tend to have less commitment (especially among men), satisfaction, and quality in the marriage.

29. Joshua R. Goldstein, "The Leveling of Divorce in the United States," *Demography* 36, no. 3 (August 1999): 410. "Divorce rates peak during the fourth year for both first marriages and remarriages," http://ccutrona.public.iastate.edu/psych592a /articles/Goldstein_1999.pdf.

30. Andrew J. Cherlin, "In the Season of Marriage, a Question. Why Bother?," *New York Times Sunday Review,* April 27, 2013, www.nytimes.com/2013/04/28/opinion/sunday/why-do -people-still-bother-to-marry.html?_r=0.

31. Rose McDermott, James H. Fowler, and Nicholas A. Christakis, "Breaking Up Is Hard to Do, Unless Everyone Else Is Doing It Too: Social Network Effects on Divorce in a Longitudinal Sample" (working paper, October 18, 2009), 38, http://papers.ssrn.com/sol3/papers.cfm?abstract_id= 1490708.

32. Scott Stanley, e-mail message to authors, October 23, 2013. The data he references on baby boomers is from Susan L. Brown and I-Fen Lin, "The Gray Divorce Revolution: Rising Divorce Among Middle-Aged and Older Adults, 1990–2010," *Journals of Gerontology Series B: Psychological Sciences and Social Sciences* 67, no. 6 (2012): 731–41, http://ncfmr.bgsu.edu/pdf/Susan%20 L.%20Brown/file108701.pdf.

33. Interestingly, Dr. Stanley's study also reviewed several other cohabitation studies and found that people who are "more traditionally religious are less likely to cohabit prior to marriage."

34. Andrew Cherlin, "Demographic Trends in the United States: A Review of Research in the 2000s," *Journal of Marriage and Family* 72, no. 3 (June 2010): 403–19, www.ncbi.nlm.nih.gov /pmc/articles/PMC3293163. "Nearly all studies suggest that the lifetime probability of [marriage] disruption is between 40% and 50%." He includes Drs. Raley, Bumpass, Schoen, Stevenson, and others as references.

35. Teresa Castro Martin and Larry L. Bumpass, "Recent Trends in Marital Disruption," *Demography* 26, no. 1 (February 1989): 49, www.jstor.org/stable/2061492. They estimate a 56 percent first-marriage divorce rate from the census of June 1985.

36. From the 1980s projections of a 50 percent average divorce rate, the average projection today is 40 to 50 percent—in other

words, 45 percent on average. That means researchers' projections have only come down about 10 percent, but the actual crude divorce rate has dropped 32 percent. (Note: up until 2009, the last year we have good comparison data, the refined divorce rate dropped 28 percent.) If the projections had followed anywhere close to the same trend, demographers would be predicting more like a 34 percent divorce rate for a newly married couple.

37. Paul Amato, phone interview with the authors, February 19, 2013.

38. Dana Rotz, "Why Have Divorce Rates Fallen? The Role of Women's Age at Marriage" (working paper, Mathematica Policy Research Inc., Harvard University, 2011), http://papers.ssrn .com/sol3/papers.cfm?abstract_id=1960017.

39. Dana Rotz, e-mail message to authors, May 29, 2013.

40. Scott Stanley, personal meeting with author, Denver, CO, January 10, 2013.

41. The study surveyed 1,304 married people—652 married couples—over the course of 2011 and 2012. To keep the surveys independent, anonymous, and as candid as possible, each person took the survey separately from their spouse. The spouses did not see each other's surveys. There were two different types of data sets. The first type were independent surveys, conducted during 2011 and 2012 either on paper or with direct-response keypads with 796 people (398 married couples) in group meeting places with a high concentration of married couples, including a church worship service, marriage conferences, a cruise for married couples, and weekend retreats. Among these independent surveys, largely of church-goers (and probably including a disproportionate number of struggling marriages), 34 percent were very happy, 37 percent happy, and 29 percent struggling. The second type of data set was a nationally representative survey conducted for us by the

research firm Decision Analyst with 508 married people (254 married couples) between March 23, 2012, and April 2, 2012. Although the survey was nationally representative for demographics such as age, race, and geographical area, it was not representative for marital happiness. We had to inflate the number of struggling couples to get a statistically significant (large enough) sample. So we tried to come relatively close to the percentages we'd found in the independent surveys. Within the Decision Analyst survey sample, 39 percent were very happy, 38 percent happy, and 22 percent struggling. See the memo in the research section of www.shaunti.com by survey designer Dr. Chuck Cowan for *The Surprising Secrets of Highly Happy Marriages* for a further explanation of our methodology.

42. These are the results of our independent surveys and do not include the Decision Analyst numbers. As noted above, that survey was not nationally representative for marital happiness.

43. Smith et al., "General Social Surveys."

44. The last year currently available for viewing on the GSS website (as of this writing) is 2008. The happiness percentage for married people in 2008 resembled the 2012 numbers: "very happy" was 62 percent, "pretty happy" was 35 percent, and "not too happy" was 3 percent (numbers rounded up).

45. Glenn, "With This Ring," 36, http://blog.fatherhood.org /with-this-ring-survey. From appendix B, "Technical Description of Survey": "The survey for this report was designed to be representative of the United States resident population age 18 and older and was conducted by telephone by the Office of Survey Research at the University of Texas–Austin in December of 2003 and January and February of 2004.... The response rate was 89 percent according to the most commonly used method of calculating response rates for telephone surveys (number of interviews/number of interviews + refusals), and there were 1,503 completed interviews. The questionnaire was

designed by Dr. Norval Glenn in consultation with advisors at the National Fatherhood Initiative."

46. Despite our many requests for more detail, this study was one of the very few on which we were forced to rely on abstracts and articles and were not able to get closer access to the study or researchers. However, because GfK is a credible survey company and this survey was showing a different and lower number than the other studies, we felt it was important to include it as a counterpoint. Here is the citation information and methodology: Michele Kimball, "Poll: Most Marriages Are Happy," Divorce360.com, www.divorce360.com/divorce-articles /statistics/us/poll-most-marriages-are-happy.aspx?artid=268. "The poll was conducted by the independent research firm for Divorce360.com. GfK Roper polled more than 1,500 people in September. The polling sample was made up of about 55 percent women and 45 percent men. The margin of error for the study is plus or minus 2.6 percent." The abstract did not say the year, but from the summary, it looks as though it was 2008.

47. Note that these numbers total only 95 percent. Because (as noted above) this was one of few studies for which, despite many requests, we were unable to get direct access to the study and researchers, we are forced to rely on published information from the sponsor of the study. That published information does not provide full details, including what categories make up the missing 5 percent.

48. Anderson, *Beyond a House Divided,* 106–7. Matthew St. John at Knights of Columbus provided the following additional information on how the Knights of Columbus / Marist National Poll July 2010 survey was conducted: "This survey of 2,029 adults was conducted July 9 through July 13, 2010. Adults eighteen years of age and older residing in the continental United States were interviewed by telephone. Telephone numbers were selected based upon a list of telephone exchanges from throughout the nation. The exchanges were selected to

ensure that each region was represented in proportion to its population. To increase coverage, this landline sample was supplemented by respondents reached through random dialing of cell phone numbers. The two samples were then combined and balanced to reflect the US Census results for age, gender, income, race, and region. Results are statistically significant within plus or minus 2.2 percentage points. There are 485 Catholics. (Knights of Columbus is a Catholic organization.) Results for this subset are statistically significant within plus or minus 4.5 percentage points. The error margin increases for cross-tabulations."

49. Survey of Marital Generosity, 2010–2011. Special data run from Brad Wilcox for Shaunti Feldhahn to cross tabulate by marital happiness categories, August 28, 2013. The survey was conducted with 2,230 married men and women between the ages of eighteen and fifty-five who had children at home. The logistic regression model also adjusted for participants' age, education, household income, and race/ethnicity. Although couples were grouped in similar categories to my *Surprising Secrets of Highly Happy Marriages* study, since this was a different survey conducted in a different way, I have titled the resulting categories "very happy," "happy," and "less than happy" to distinguish the results from my own categories of "highly happy," "mostly happy," and "so-so and struggling."

50. Christine Johnson et al., "Marriage in Oklahoma: 2001 Baseline Statewide Survey on Marriage and Divorce," Oklahoma Marriage Initiative. Findings for this report are based on telephone interviews conducted with a statewide sample of 2,323 adults. The sample consisted of 2,020 adults from randomly selected households and 303 randomly selected current Medicaid clients. Based on the total sample, one can say with 95 percent confidence that the error attributable to sampling and other random effects is plus or minus 2.02 percentage points.

51. The GfK Roper poll is an example of a survey that asked a much more specific question about what percent of the time the marriage was happy. This is probably why the number (75 percent) was a bit lower and perhaps more realistic.

52. In addition to the Marist and National Fatherhood Initiative surveys noted here, other polls have found similar numbers. For example, an official CBS News poll, "Love and Marriage," has found that since they began conducting the survey in 1995, 90 to 93 percent of married Americans would marry their spouse all over again. (CBS News Poll, "Love and Marriage: January 29–31, 2010," www.cbsnews.com/htdocs/pdf/Poll_Jan10d Love.pdf.)

53. Marist Poll, "Do You Think You Married the Right Person, or Not?," http://maristpoll.marist.edu/86-most-americans -hitched-to-the-right-wagon-but. Nature of the sample: This survey of 1,004 US residents was conducted June 17 through June 24 of 2010. Residents eighteen years of age and older were interviewed by telephone. Telephone numbers were selected based upon a list of telephone exchanges from throughout the nation. The exchanges were selected to ensure that each region was represented in proportion to its popula- tion. To increase coverage, this landline sample was supple- mented by respondents reached through random dialing of cell phone numbers. The two samples were then combined. Results are statistically significant at plus or minus 3.0 percent. There are 530 residents who are married. The results for this subset are statistically significant at plus or minus 4.5 percent.

54. Glenn, "With This Ring," 34.

55. Linda J. Waite et al., *Does Divorce Make People Happy? Findings from a Study of Unhappy Marriages,* Institute for American Values, 2002, 4, 11, https://docs.google.com/viewer?url=http: //americanvalues.org/catalog/pdfs/does_divorce_make_people _happy.pdf.

56. There has been some lively debate among sociologists and psychologists about whether the Waite study in some way focuses more on couples experiencing easier-to-solve marital discord rather than deeper marital distress. (See S. R. H. Beach and F. D. Fincham, "Spontaneous Remission of Marital Discord: A Simmering Debate with Profound Implications for Family Psychology," *Family Psychologist* 19 [2003]: 11–13.) However, in our basic review of Waite's study and supporting material that she e-mailed to us directly, it is clear that her methodology was rigorous and that she is including couples of *all* categories, including couples whom we would consider to be in marital distress. Furthermore, her analysis was based on how the couples themselves rated their marriages over time; she did not assign them rankings. So although we are aware of the controversy (in part spurred by the question of whether the benefits of sticking with it are "too good to be true"), in our judgment the Waite study appears to be well done.

57. Waite et al., *Does Divorce Make People Happy?*, 5.

58. Waite et al., *Does Divorce Make People Happy?*, 5.

59. The following are results from currently married persons who at some point thought their marriage was in trouble and considered divorce, who were asked "Are you glad you are still together?" Among those married seven years or less, 79 percent were glad, 15 percent were unsure or had mixed feelings, and only 6 percent were not glad. Among those married eight years or more, 95 to 97 percent were glad (depending on number of years married), 1 to 5 percent were unsure/mixed, and 0 to 2 percent were not glad. (See endnote 50 in this book and page 28, table 22, of the report.)

60. Unpublished song by Danny Oertli, November 17, 2010. Used with the permission of Danny Oertli.

61. The article was about the CDC's newly released National Survey of Family Growth data from 2006 to 2010, declaring that 48 percent of women were divorced by their twentieth

anniversary—without mentioning that those numbers were entirely of women who married very young. For an adjustment to those numbers, see the FAQ section.

62. This chapter will focus solely on churchgoers, rather than those attending worship services of other faiths. Although several studies (including my own) surveyed those attending Jewish or Muslim services, for example, the sample size was in many cases too small to be statistically significant. However, from what we can tell from the smaller numbers, these conclusions appear to apply to those who attend worship services in other religious settings as well.

63. Some studies, for example, look at worship attendance for any faith; others just look at Christians. Some define "regular attendance" as weekly; others as twice a month or more. Other studies simply look at "religious affiliation"—maybe with attendance, maybe without. Still others bypass worship attendance and study other actions such as praying together, studying the Bible, and discussing God's will in marriage. And there are several studies, such as Barna's, that look at religious beliefs, not practices. Some of the confusion in researching this topic has also revolved around the publication dates. Several high-profile academic studies to come out in the last five to seven years are still analyzing NSFH data from 1987 to 1994.

64. Special Report for Shaunti Feldhahn, 2008 OmniPoll, Barna Group, Ventura, CA, 2013.

65. Since the Barna Group wasn't studying church attendance per se, they didn't ask questions such as "How often do you attend services?" Instead, they asked something like "Have you done one of these things in the last seven days?" with one option being whether the person had been to church. Although that will include a few extra people (those who were in a church out of curiosity or at a wedding, for example), it will also exclude a few regular attenders (for example, those who were on vacation

and missed church that week). So it still is probably a fairly good proxy for those who actually attend church regularly.

66. Barna classifies those who hold specific beliefs as "evangelical" (respondents were not asked to describe themselves as such). Specifically, the Barna Group says evangelicals are defined as "people who said they have made a personal commitment to Jesus Christ that is still important in their life today and who also indicated they believe that when they die they will go to Heaven because they had confessed their sins and had accepted Jesus Christ as their savior." This group also includes those who "say their faith is very important in their life today; believing they have a personal responsibility to share their religious beliefs about Christ with non-Christians; believing that Satan exists; believing that eternal salvation is possible only through grace, not works; believing that Jesus Christ lived a sinless life on earth; asserting that the Bible is accurate in all that it teaches; and describing God as the all-knowing, all-powerful, perfect deity who created the universe and still rules it today. Being classified as an evangelical is not dependent upon church attendance or the denominational affiliation of the church attended." (See www.barna.org/barna-update/family-kids/42 -new-marriage-and-divorce-statistics-released#.UsDeWPRDtng.)

67. Another area of good news has to do with the rate of marriage itself. While sociologists continue to be concerned by decreasing marriage rates (in part due to people living together), that trend is also better in the average church. According to our tabulations of Barna's 2013 data, while the overall rate of marriage did decline, 79 percent of weekly church attenders are or have been married compared to just 66 percent of nonattenders.

68. W. Bradford Wilcox and Elizabeth Williamson, "The Cultural Contradictions of Mainline Family Ideology and Practice," in *American Religions and the Family: How Faith Traditions Cope with Modernization and Democracy,* ed. Don S. Browning and

David A. Clairmont (New York: Columbia University Press, 2006).

69. Unlike most other surveys, this survey asked questions designed to get at nuances about attendance and affiliation. The couples were asked their religious preference and how often they attended a religious service, among other things. If the respondents answered Protestant, they were then asked, "What specific denomination is that?" This kind of detail tends to illuminate even clearer patterns about drops in the divorce rate by attendance than those found in the Barna survey (which, as noted, was not designed to focus on nuances about attendance).

70. James A. Sweet and Larry L. Bumpass, "The National Survey of Families and Households—Waves 1 and 2: Data Description and Documentation," Center for Demography and Ecology, University of Wisconsin–Madison, 1996, www.ssc.wisc.edu /nsfh/home.htm. The first two waves of more than thirteen thousand people were completed between 1987 and 1994, with ten thousand follow-up interviews in the second wave. Many different researchers have analyzed significant samples from the initial wave and/or follow-up interviews (from "Sample Design," www.ssc.wisc.edu/nsfh/design.htm).

71. The NSFH/Wilcox analysis clearly found a much larger drop in divorce among those who attend church (compared to those who don't) than the Barna Group did. The real answer today is probably somewhere between the two. The NSFH is comprised of older data, but the survey was also much larger and is considered more precise than the Barna survey, particularly on this topic. Barna surveys, as noted earlier, did not ask participants whether they regularly attended church or did other religious activities but simply asked if they had been in church the last seven days, thirty days, and so on. (Our tabulations for this book included those who had been in church the last seven days.) When we compare the Barna and NSFH data to other

studies we have, it appears that the drop today is likely somewhere in between the Barna average drop of 27 percent and the NSFH/Wilcox average drop of 50 percent.

72. W. Bradford Wilcox, "Is Religion an Answer? Marriage, Fatherhood, and the Male Problematic," Research Brief No. 11 (New York: Institute for American Values, 2008), www.american values.org/search/item.php?id=20.

73. Although the "Cultural Contradictions" study itself lists the reductions by various divorce groups and denominations, it does not list one final overall average for all Christians. In correspondence with us and in his paper "Is Religion an Answer?," Dr. Wilcox repeatedly referred to an average drop of 50 percent before controlling for other factors, and an average drop of 35 percent after controlling for those factors.

74. One interesting finding was that *before* controlling for socioeconomic factors, mainline Protestants had lower rates of divorce than various evangelical groups that, traditionally, have had a greater stigma against divorce, such as evangelical Protestants and black Protestants. In "Is Religion an Answer?" Dr. Wilcox explained that "evangelical Protestants and black Protestants face somewhat higher divorce rates because they are more likely to hail from working-class and poor communities where economic struggles often stress marriages."

75. Margaret L. Vaaler, Christopher G. Ellison, and Daniel A. Powers, "Religious Influences on the Risk of Marital Dissolution," *Journal of Marriage and Family* 71 (November 2009).

76. Christopher G. Ellison, professor of sociology, University of Texas–San Antonio, e-mail message to authors, April 28, 2013.

77. Gritzon, "Super Composite." The Family Needs Survey is highly specialized, asking church members 180 questions to understand their degree of faith commitment, how their family relationships work, what their habits are, and so on. See www .familylife.com/FNS.

78. In part because of the demographic makeup of some of the churches, and in part because it was a long survey that young couples with kids couldn't take the time to complete, 48 percent of survey takers were over age fifty and 68 percent were over age forty.

79. David McLaughlin, "The Role of the Man in the Family," David McLaughlin audio series, www.discipleshiplibrary.com /search.php?a=1&e=0&m=0&n=0&p=0&s=series&t= SERIES&st=series&ss=Role%20of%20the%20Man%20 in%20the%20Family.

80. Special analysis from "When Baby Makes Three: How Parenthood Makes Life Meaningful and How Marriage Makes Parenthood Bearable," *The State of Our Unions 2011* (Charlottesville, VA: National Marriage Project at the University of Virginia, 2011), 31–32, figure 13, www.stateofourunions .org/2011/when-baby-makes-three.php. Special analysis of couples in each happiness category, for Shaunti Feldhahn.

81. Here's a bit more detail: Where 97 percent of married people had happy marriages and 68 percent said they were very happy, that 68 percent average wasn't nearly as informative as its parts. It turned out that among those who never attend religious services, only 52 percent were very happy, whereas among those who attended regularly (at least monthly), the number was 72 percent or higher.

82. Peter J. Larson and David H. Olson, "Spiritual Beliefs and Marriage: A National Survey Based on ENRICH," *Family Psychologist* 20, no. 2 (2004): 4–8, www.apa.org/divisions /div43/news/NewsArchives/Spring04TFPfinal.pdf.

83. Robert Lewis and Tim and Lea Lundy, *Marriage Oneness,* FamilyLife (2010), www.marriageonenessprofile.com.

84. Marriage Oneness Survey of 7,700 married individuals (3,850 couples) tabulated by PREPARE/ENRICH, October 10, 2013. Surveys conducted as part of the "Marriage Oneness Profiles" for participants in the *Marriage Oneness* video study by Family-

Life (http://lifeready.com/marriageoneness/). Levels of closeness are based on a validated and robust couple typology scoring algorithm developed by PREPARE/ENRICH. It requires both individuals to rate their relationship healthy across a range of the Marriage Oneness topics in order to be categorized as "highly connected."

85. Leo Averbach, "The High Failure Rate of Second and Third Marriages: Why Are Second and Third Marriages More Likely to Fail?," *Psychology Today,* for Mark Banschick, *The Intelligent Divorce,* February 6, 2012, www.psychologytoday.com/blog /the-intelligent-divorce/201202/ the-high-failure-rate-second-and-third-marriages.

86. Jennifer Baker, e-mail message to authors, May 30, 2013.

87. The citation was listed as "US Bureau of the Census, 2006, Statistical Abstract of the U.S. (122nd ed.)," but as noted, those statistics are simply not listed in this publication.

88. For example, there were two longitudinal studies done during the height of the worst divorce-rate years to look at issues such as the impact of divorce on children, one by Dr. Mavis Hetherington and another by Dr. Judith Wallerstein. See E. Mavis Hetherington and John Kelly, *For Better or For Worse: Divorce Reconsidered* (New York: Norton, 2002), 262; and Judith S. Wallerstein, Julia M. Lewis, and Sandra Blakeslee, *The Unexpected Legacy of Divorce: A 25 Year Landmark Study* (New York: Hyperion, 2000).

Neither was designed or intended to get a handle on the divorce rate, especially since they were engineering their sample in order to get a very high proportion of divorced families, with a specific number of children, at specific ages, and so on, so they could study the impact of divorce. Hetherington ended up tracking 450 families over four different longitudinal "waves" in Virginia (each wave had smaller sample sizes, with 144 families in one wave and 121 families in another wave). Wallerstein's study was smaller, with 121 children from 60 families. Both studies started at a great time to consider the impact of divorce on children, since they were conducted during the highest divorce-rate years (Hetherington's study initially started in 1972, and Wallerstein's started in 1971), and both went twenty years or more. Although both found an extremely high divorce rate (around six in ten or higher) among the participants who had been remarried, it is important to know that these studies were designed with samples that would deliver insight about the impact of divorce on children and thus not appropriate to draw conclusions about the national divorce rate or the redivorce rate.

89. For example, Drs. Larry Bumpass and Teresa Castro Martin in 1989 projected that, based on the 1985 Current Population Survey, 56 percent of first marriages would end in divorce or separation by the forty-year anniversary mark. Overall, they figured second marriages had a 25 percent greater chance of breaking up. Divorce numbers quickly began declining again, so those projections were moot, but it is possible that readers could have misunderstood those as saying they had found those actual numbers.

90. Cherlin, "Demographic Trends in the United States."

91. Kreider and Ellis, "Number, Timing, and Duration: 2009."

92. Note that in chapter 2, we had enough first-marriage divorce data for couples to know that 72 percent of *marriages* were still intact. Here, we refer to 71 percent of *women* being in marriages that are still intact. Since remarriage data is sparser, in this chapter we will be focusing on the divorce rates of women, specifically (not couples), which is the only way we can compare first-, second-, and third-marriage divorce rates.

93. We can see this, in fact, by comparing the numbers for men and women. Since women are more likely to live longer and thus more likely to be widowed, we would expect fewer of their marriages to still be intact than among men—which is exactly what we see. Among men in their second marriage, the percent

of those marriages still intact is much higher: 78 percent! Just 22 percent of these men are no longer married to their second wife.

94. Larry Bumpass has long been a respected expert in the field of marriage and divorce research, publishing several studies, including a few on the subject of remarriage. Because Dr. Bumpass has retired from teaching, most of the divorce and remarriage data is dated from earlier surveys, during the highest-risk years, and thus doesn't give a current snapshot of today's situation. But one of his studies did find a *pattern* that seems to match the data we do have that is more recent, so his conclusion is likely to be still valid today.

     Using 1985 Current Population Survey data, Dr. Bumpass estimated that remarriages generally had a risk of divorce that was 25 percent greater than first marriages. But nearly all that risk came in the first few years. Once a couple in a remarriage had made it five years, the increased chance of divorce was only four percentage points (23 percent for first marriages versus 27 percent for second marriages). The study also found that once "age at first marriage" was accounted for, the difference between first- and second-marriage divorce rates disappears. (See Castro Martin and Bumpass, "Recent Trends," 41–47.)

95. Alison Aughinbaugh, Omar Robles, and Hugette Sun, "Marriage and Divorce: Patterns by Gender, Race, and Educational Attainment," *Monthly Labor Review* (October 2013): table 3, section "Among Those Who Remarried After Divorce," www.bls.gov/opub/mlr/2013/article/marriage-and -divorce-patterns-by-gender-race-and-educational-attainment .htm. The BLS examined a specific cohort in the well-known longitudinal study National Longitudinal Survey of Youth 1979 (NLSY79).

96. Matthew D. Bramlett and William D. Mosher, "Cohabitation, Marriage, Divorce, and Remarriage in the United States," *Vital and Health Statistics* 23, no. 22 (July 2002), www.cdc.gov/nchs

/data/series/sr_23/sr23_022.pdf. Compare table 21 on page 55
with table 41 on page 83 (0.33 versus 0.39).

97. By ten years of marriage, 33 percent of those in their first
marriage had divorced, compared to 39 percent of those in their
second marriage. (As noted, these rates are high because this
study heavily surveyed those who married young. An adjustment for a more representative age of marriage is discussed in
the FAQ section.)

98. Goldstein, "Leveling of Divorce," 410–11.

99. Krista K. Payne, First Divorces in the U.S., 2008, Family
Profiles FP-10-06 (Bowling Green, OH: National Center for
Family and Marriage Research, Bowling Green University,
2011), www.bgsu.edu/content/dam/BGSU/college-of-arts
-and-sciences/NCFMR/documents/FP/FP-10-06.pdf.

100. See Shaunti Feldhahn, *The Surprising Secrets of Highly Happy
Marriages: The Little Things That Make a Big Difference*
(Colorado Springs: Multnomah, 2013).

101. For more, see chapter 3 in Feldhahn, *Surprising Secrets,* or the
research section of www.shaunti.com.

102. Other evidence of this is the polls that show 93 to 95 percent of
married people saying they married the right person and would
marry them all over again (see chapter 3). Only 5 to 7 percent
felt that they didn't and wouldn't, and it seems reasonable to
infer that those couples are more likely to be the ones encounter-
ing bigger, systemic issues. But if the overall divorce rate ends up
being around 30 percent, many more than that 5 to 7 percent
end up divorcing. Thus, we can infer that *many* of the others
who split are *not* as likely to be doing so because of big, systemic
issues.

103. Specifically, the Decision Analyst survey for *The Surprising
Secrets of Highly Happy Marriages,* not the independent surveys
for the same book. On that survey, 22 percent of couples were
struggling, compared to 29 percent in our internal surveys. As
explained in endnote 41 above, the "very happy," "happy," and

"struggling" percentages on the Decision Analyst survey were engineered to ensure we would have a statistically valid (large enough) sample of struggling couples to analyze. The final groupings were in the same ballpark as our internal surveys: 39 percent "highly happy," 38 percent "happy," 22 percent "struggling." We are using this survey instead of our internal surveys for this particular analysis because the technology behind it allowed us to get a precise comparison between individuals and couples, where the independent surveys carried a possibility of a few percentage points' error either way. (The fact that the Decision Analyst percentages were engineered should have little impact on the analysis of how many individuals described themselves as happy versus how many couples did, once the answers of both spouses were taken into account.)

104. The data about the percentages of men and women who have these various emotional needs comes from *The Surprising Secrets of Highly Happy Marriages, For Women Only,* and *For Men Only.*

105. Sam Roberts, "Divorce After 50 Grows More Common," *New York Times,* September 20, 2013, www.nytimes.com/2013/09 /22/fashion/weddings/divorce-after-50-grows-more-common .html?emc=eta1&_r=0.

106. Janean Chun, "Bert and John Jacobs, Life Is Good: From Living in a Van to Running a $100 Million Company," *Huffington Post,* March 21, 2012, www.huffingtonpost.com/2012/03/21 /bert-john-jacobs-life-is-good_n_1345033.html.

107. Assuming, in our simplistic example, that the number of marriages in the church stayed exactly the same over the thirty years and that they were starting from no divorces. Neither of these is going to be true in the real world, of course, but this at least shows why the divorces-as-a-percent-of-marriages-each-year does not give us the divorce rate.

108. The ratio of approximately two marriages to one divorce can be found as early as the 1975 to 1977 time period. See Arthur J.

Norton and Louisa F. Miller, "Marriage, Divorce, and Remarriage in the 1990's," *Current Population Reports* P23-180 (October 1992): 2, table A, www.census.gov/hhes/socdemo /marriage/data/cps/p23-180/p23-180.pdf.

109. The National Vital Statistics System in 2011 listed the number of marriages nationwide as 2,118,000 out of 311,591,917 people, for a rate of 6.8 per 1,000 total population. The number for divorces nationally reached 877,000, but out of only 246,273,366 people, which would be a rate of 3.6 per 1,000 total population, but they used different populations for each category. See www.cdc.gov /nchs/nvss/marriage_divorce_tables.htm.

110. Rotz, "Why Have Divorce Rates Fallen?"

111. Manning, Brown, and Payne, "Two Decades," 22.

112. Aughinbaugh, Robles, and Sun, "Marriage and Divorce."

113. Casey E. Copen et al., "First Marriages in the United States: Data from the 2006–2010 National Survey of Family Growth," *National Health Statistics Reports* 49 (March 22, 2012), www .cdc.gov/nchs/data/nhsr/nhsr049.pdf.

114. For example, Shaunti looked at how much the divorce rate improved for those who married at age twenty-five and older compared to those who married at ages twenty to twenty-four at each of the other anniversary thresholds. Then she applied that same improvement for the twentieth-anniversary mark to estimate what the divorce rate might have been for that group if the survey had included people married long enough to reach that mark. In fact, that improvement had increased for each anniversary (the divorce rate was 26 percent lower at the fifth anniversary, 29 percent lower at the tenth, and 33 percent lower at the fifteenth). With a three- to four-point improvement each time, it could easily have been 37 percent lower at the twentieth, so we felt it was conservative to assume it would stay at 33 percent for the twentieth-anniversary mark as well. Using a 33 percent lower divorce rate than the twenty to twenty-four age group gives us a 30 percent divorce and 70 percent survival rate.

115. For example, Dr. Betsey Stevenson did a reanalysis of the 2004 Census SIPP data because she found a discrepancy with the data that caused a higher divorce rate than she thought probable. See Betsey Stevenson and Justin Wolfers, "Trends in Marital Stability," in *Research Handbook on the Economics of Family Law,* ed. Lloyd R. Cohen and Joshua D. Wright (Northampton, MA: Edward Elgar, 2011), 102.

116. Francesca Adler-Baeder, e-mail message to authors, October 12, 2013.

117. Note that number (34.5 percent) is out of the total population, but since 94 percent have been married, that is still very close to the real figure. If the table showed those divorced *out of ever married,* the number would be 37 percent.

118. Norval D. Glenn, *Closed Hearts, Closed Minds: The Textbook Story of Marriage* (New York: Institute for American Values, 1997), 3, http://americanvalues.org/catalog/pdfs/closedhearts .pdf.

119. David Olson, phone interview with the authors, October 25, 2013.

120. Brown and Lin, "Gray Divorce."

121. Betsey Stevenson, e-mail message to authors, April 26, 2013. Dr. Stevenson indicated the "ACS provided divorce numbers for a short period, but they aren't comparable to public records like vital statistics. ACS reports overestimate divorce rates. They are based on asking people if they've gotten divorced in the past year and it looks like people are answering over a broader time frame (for instance saying 'yes' even if their divorce isn't quite finalized)."

122. Another study published in late 2013 by the Bureau of Labor Statistics (BLS) found a higher rate of divorce among baby boomers' first marriages as well. Again, these results look somewhat more depressing; but if you look closely, you notice that this study is a longitudinal study, using a very narrow segment of the highest-risk group of people (baby boomers born

from 1957 to 1964). Unfortunately, this study came out just as this book was going into production, so we did not have a chance to fully analyze it. (See Aughinbaugh, Robles, and Sun, "Marriage and Divorce.") But as we referenced Scott Stanley, pointing out in chapter 2, "Divorce is increasing rapidly among those older than fifty, but the great increase is among those who are remarried and/or in shorter duration marriages."

123. Part of why Dr. Bumpass's percentages are so high is because he included separation in his estimates. (See Castro Martin and Bumpass, "Recent Trends.")

124. Robert Schoen and Nicola Standish, "The Retrenchment of Marriage: Results from Marital Status Life Tables for the United States, 1995," *Population and Development Review* 27 (2001): 553–63.

125. Paul Amato, phone interview with the authors, February 19, 2013. Dr. Amato also mentioned that Schoen increased his projection to 45 percent in 2006, using data from 2000; but this has not been updated since and, again, does not distinguish between death and divorce.

126. As we were putting the finishing touches on the book, we talked to an expert at the University of Minnesota, Dr. Sheela Kennedy, who even projected a divorce *increase.* In an interview, she shared the conclusion from her paper that if one took "2010 as the standard population, the age-standardized divorce rate rose 40 percent between 1980 and 2008." See also Kennedy and Ruggles, "Breaking Up Is Hard to Count." (Sheela Kennedy, e-mail correspondence with authors, October 25, 2013.)

127. Glenn Stanton, interview with the author at Focus on the Family, Colorado Springs, CO, January 9, 2013.

128. Andrew J. Cherlin, *Marriage, Divorce, Remarriage* (Cambridge, MA: Harvard University Press, 1992), 29.

129. Bramlett and Mosher, "Cohabitation," 55, table 21.

130. The Survey of Marital Generosity has produced some interesting and positive findings. This nationally representative survey

interviewed over sixteen hundred married couples. The Science of Generosity at the University of Notre Dame is funding the survey with Dr. Brad Wilcox as principal investigator. In addition to other factors, Wilcox, along with Jeffrey Dew at Utah State, specifically examined how likely people thought they were to divorce, a factor the researchers labeled "divorce proneness."

The researchers found that among couples where both the husband and the wife attended church regularly, only 4 percent of women and 6 percent of men thought they were at risk of divorce! Compare these figures to 13 percent and 21 percent among women and men where neither person attended church regularly. In other words, when couples attended church regularly, they are 70 percent less likely to feel that they will be a statistic.

See also *The State of Our Unions 2011* and Jeffrey P. Dew and W. Bradford Wilcox, "Generosity and the Maintenance of Marital Quality," *Journal of Marriage and Family* 75, no. 5 (October 2013): 1218–28. Received copy in personal e-mail with Jeffrey Dew, June 16, 2013.

131. Bradley R. E. Wright, *Christians Are Hate-Filled Hypocrites… and Other Lies You've Been Told: A Sociologist Shatters Myths from the Secular and Christian Media* (Minneapolis: Bethany, 2010), 133. Dr. Wright also wrote about the divorce rate falling in his most recent book, *Upside: Surprising Good News About the State of Our World.* He was also kind enough to share his refined divorce rate chart in an e-mail to the authors on May 27, 2013. Information on his books and articles can be found at http://brewright.com.

132. The first study was sent to us by Dr. Mahoney herself as an attachment in a personal e-mail on May 20, 2013. (See Annette Mahoney, "Religion in Families, 1999–2009: A Relational Spirituality Framework," *Journal of Marriage and Family* 72, no. 4 [August 2010]: 805–27, www.ncbi.nlm.nih.gov/pmc/articles

/PMC3219420.) Note that she discussed what a divorce rate might be for those who are religious, if the starting-point divorce rate was 50 percent. She noted the calculation she did in the study is not to be taken literally, as many readers have done, but she was trying out numbers with a presumed 50 percent divorce rate just to see in general what the effect of church attendance would be on divorce. (See A. Mahoney et al., "Religion in the Home in the 1980s and 1990s: A Meta-Analytic Review and Conceptual Analysis of Religion, Marriage, and Parenting," *Journal of Family Psychology* 15, no. 4 [December 2001]: 559–96.) Dr. Mahoney has created a website (www .bgsu.edu/departments/psych/spirituality/) for public use entitled the Psychology of Spirituality and Family Relationships that lists these two studies.

133. Gritzon, "Super Composite."
134. By and large, those who prayed and read the Bible were just as likely to have been divorced as those who hadn't. But since all survey takers were *in a church* and were committed enough to take this extensive, lengthy survey, that signal of commitment is probably trumping any other factor in the actual divorce rate. Also, as noted earlier, this survey ended up capturing a higher percentage of baby boomers (who have a much higher divorce rate than those older and younger), which is probably also skewing the results.